The Dynamics Party Support

Cohort-Analyzing Party Identification

PHILIP E. CONVERSE

Volume 35
SAGE LIBRARY OF
SOCIAL RESEARCH

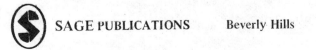

SAGE PUBLICATIONS   Beverly Hills   London

For information address:

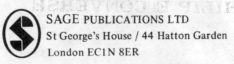

SAGE PUBLICATIONS, INC.
275 South Beverly Drive
Beverly Hills, California 90212

SAGE PUBLICATIONS LTD
St George's House / 44 Hatton Garden
London EC1N 8ER

Printed in the United States of America

Library of Congress Cataloging in Publication Data

Converse, Philip E   1928-
   The dynamics of party support.

   (Sage library of social research ; v. 35)
   Bibliography: p. 169
   Includes index.
   1. Party affiliation—United States—Longitudinal
studies.   I. Title.
JK2271.C66   329'.02   76-40523
ISBN 0-8039-0727-3
ISBN 0-8039-0728-1 pbk.

FIRST PRINTING

CONTENTS

FOREWORD

This little book is something of an accident. Although it now masquerades between covers, it was begun some years ago as a short article. Indeed, it reports among other things a number of analyses developed in connection with the preparation of *The American Voter* over fifteen years ago, but which were not included in that volume because the clinching results did not come along until that manuscript was nearly final, and lodged in preliminary form with a publisher already horrified at its length. I was prompted to return to the subject in the early 1970s out of perplexity at some of the conclusions being arrived at by secondary analysts of our data and cognate series. As a piece of inquiry unsullied by any research funding, it was consigned to the category of nights-and-Sundays work, and the originally projected short article was thereby never properly rounded out. It would probably never have been finished but for the freedoms provided by a sabbatical leave, and if in the interim it has become swollen and outsized, it is because I have had far too much time to think about the subject and far too little time to do the actual writing.

In this connection, I would like to express my deep gratitude to the John Simon Guggenheim Memorial Foundation for providing the major extensions of routine sabbatical support which permitted completion of the manuscript, even though my primary research efforts as a Guggenheim Fellow were devoted to quite a different enterprise.

My intellectual debts lie in such abundant number that complete retrieval seems impossible. In the deeper background, enormous credit belongs to my *American Voter* colleagues: to Angus Campbell, who among other relevant contributions originated the concept and measurement of party identification; to Warren E. Miller, whose intellectual stimulation and administrative encouragement have been at the bottom of all my work; and to Donald E. Stokes, who continued to pursue the subject of cohort inference with me over the years.

I also owe special thanks to Ronald Atkinson and Russell Dalton, who were the most persevering among a number of graduate students in the early 1970s demanding to know what my evidence was for ignoring and even contradicting several conclusions which had become comfortably ensconced in the intervening literature involving cohort analyses of party identification, in the course of their seminars. It was when I failed to convince them in informal discussion, that I began to write a more carefully plotted "short article."

Finally, in the more recent foreground, let me acknowledge a debt to the members of the Social Science Research Council's Advisory and Planning Committee on Social Indicators, including James A. Davis, Stephen E. Fienberg, Leo A. Goodman, Mancur Olson, Natalie Rogoff Ramsoy, Albert J. Reiss, Jr., Arthur L. Stinchcombe, Leroy Stone and Wolfgang Zapf, and its Staff Director, Robert Parke. It was the discussions of the committee on the cohort inference problem that convinced me I should expand this manuscript to pay more attention to the general case, using the analysis of party identification merely as an example and an immediate vehicle. I want to give special thanks to Otis Dudley Duncan, Chairman of the Social Indicators Committee, both for his gems of insight on the problem, and for his kind reading of a preliminary draft of this essay on very short notice. Needless to say, any sins of commission or omission in this book remain my unique personal responsibility, as the committee's role was more inspirational than directly advisory.

October 1976   Philip E. Converse
Ann Arbor, Michigan

Chapter 1

INTRODUCTION

Few variables have been subjected to as many cohort analyses in recent years as "party identification."[1] In part, this popularity is due to the demonstrated importance of these abiding feelings of party attachments in the determination of voting choices. In part as well, the popularity is a matter of expediency. There are few time series available in sample survey data that are now as rich or as long as these measurements of partisanship. Hence this variable has, among other things, tended to become a workhorse in efforts to develop a proper methodology of cohort analysis.

There is still another reason why party identification is of uncommon interest for longitudinal study. This item, particularly as measured in Survey Research Center studies, is really not a single variable, but can profitably be treated as having two highly distinct components. One is the component of the direction of party choice, be that Democratic or Republican. The other is the strength of this attachment to either party, a variable that lumps together "strong" Democrats and "strong" Republicans at one pole, and pure independents or apoliticals at the other, with gradations of weaker partisans between.

Both the direction and the strength components, over the period for which measurements are available, show persistent static relationships with the age of respondents. Where party direction is concerned, older people have typically been relatively Republican, and younger people relatively Democratic. Similarly, age usually turns out to be the most potent demographic predictor of variations in the strength of partisanship, irrespective of the direction of party choice: older people are generally stronger partisans than younger.

What is fascinating from the point of view of cohort analysis is the possibility that these two components of the same parent variable have strikingly different dynamic backgrounds.

Whenever a static relationship is observed between age and some dependent variable like party identification, there is a fundamental dilemma of interpretation. Does the static relationship arise because of generational differences in the Mannheim (1952) sense, or because of maturational or life-cycle processes that would take place in more or less the same form within any historical generation? The distinction is a capital one, for it not only bears in the most direct way upon any theoretical understanding of the dynamics of the variable involved, but also is crucial for extrapolating from the present to the most plausible future state of affairs. That is, if the observed age relationship is generational in nature, then time is likely to be on the side of whatever deviations the young display on the variable, since older cohorts are progressively dying out in what Ryder (1965) has appropriately termed the process of "demographic metabolism," and genuine aggregate social change can be expected. If, on the other hand, the age relationship is purely a life-cycle matter, the better extrapolation is one of constancy: whereas the old are dying out, middle-aged cohorts are drifting from the "young" position to the contrasting position of the elderly, thereby producing a kind of equilibrium that leaves the aggregated population values unchanged. Given this ambiguity, the central problem of cohort analysis is well-known: with a study at a single point in time, and an observed static relationship of a dependent variable with age, there is no possible means of discriminating between the two contrasting types of dynamic effects in any conclusive empirical way. Whatever verdict the analyst may wish to render on the basis of such a single study must hinge, in a very Bayesian sense, on the introduction of side information about the variable in question or features of the historical epoch involved. In short, any substantive case must rest on contentions of relative plausibility, rather than iron-clad proof.

The static relationships between age and the two components of party identification provide stunning illustrations of this dilemma, since in both cases the competing generational and maturational interpretations have a surface plausibility. Where direction is concerned, older people may be relatively more Republican in the United States as a function of life-cycle changes: it is commonly supposed that aging breeds increased conservatism, and therefore the more conservative Republican Party should have increased appeal to voters as they grow older. On the other hand, perhaps the static age relationship is a reflection of the known succession of political periods in our electoral history: older persons were socialized in a period of Republican ascendancy before the Great Depression and Roosevelt's New Deal, whereas younger cohorts matured in a period of relative Democratic popularity.

The strength component of the party identification variable suffers a parallel ambiguity. Perhaps older people are more staunchly partisan due to a variety of obvious factors, both perceptual and social, that would be likely to reinforce the strength of any initial party preference progressively over the life cycle. Or perhaps, as Burnham (1965; 1969), Jensen (1968) and others have argued, the political ethos of grass-roots politics in an earlier epoch in this country was more ardently and unquestioningly partisan than it has been in recent years. From this point of view, the stronger partisanship of the old is simply a reflection of such change, and people who are currently middle-aged cannot be expected to show stronger partisanship as they become old. Instead, aggregate expressions of the strength of partisan preferences will decline progressively as the current older generation dies away.

In *The American Voter* we suggested contrasting verdicts as to the dynamics of the two components of the party identification measure, although at the time of writing we had but a very short span of data—mainly covering four to six years—on which to base such a discrimination. Despite the fact that conventional wisdom of the time presumed the prevalence of Republicans among the elderly to be a life-cycle product of aging and conservatism, we described the cohort behavior of the directional component in terms of historical generations (Campbell et al., 1960). On the other hand, we conjectured that the static relationship between age and strength of partisanship so clear in the data of the 1950s was a result of life-cycle gains in partisan feeling, rather than a reflection of changes associated with historical generations. Indeed, in this and subsequent publications we went considerably beyond the latter verdict taken alone, generating something of a mini-theory of the development of such identifications that seemed to test out impressively not only in the United States but on cross-national data as well (Converse, 1969).

What is perhaps the core idea in this small theory is the hypothesis that identifications intensify as a function not of age per se, but rather as a function of the length of time that the individual has felt some generalized preference for a particular party and has repetitively voted for it. In systems where party alternatives have been stable for a generation or two and only small fractions of the electorate are converted from their original party to another later in life, the age variable is so strongly correlated with the length of identification variable that it displays almost as strong a static relationship with strength of partisanship as the latter would if properly measured. However, numerous conditions can intrude to disrupt the age relationship, even when duration of identification is having its normal accumulative effect where strength of partisanship is concerned. Thus, for example, the small minority of voters who shift basic loyalties at later points in life appear to gain in strength of identification with their new parties at measurably slower rates than the young, and the older the person was chronologically at the time of change, the slower his subsequent gain rate will be. It can be seen that there is imbedded in this codicil an overtone of the aging-conservatism equation, except that it has a rather different flavor. Instead of the standard ideological proposition, it postulates that absorption of new ideas slows down with age, whatever the ideological stripe of these new ideas may be.

The important point for our immediate purposes, however, is the observation that chronological age in the life-cycle sense is only a rough surrogate for what should really be measured to account for age-related gains in partisan strength. Under recent American conditions, it is a serviceable surrogate in addressing gross trends in the total electorate. However, it should be kept in mind that when length of time identifying with a particular party is held constant, partisan strength is expected to be *negatively* correlated with age. Similarly, in new political systems or those with rapid turnover of party alternatives, there may actually be a negative zero-order correlation for total electorates between chronological age and strength of identification.[2]

The fifteen years that have elapsed since these contrasting verdicts about the two components of party identification were first set out have produced an automatic tripling of the length of the time series available for cohort analysis. Indeed, the use by some investigators of Gallup data on partisan preferences stretching back into the 1940s has extended the time frame available to us by a factor of five. It is this broadening data base that has encouraged a flourishing subliterature of cohort analyses of party identification.

Over the course of this literature, our two verdicts have endured a rather checkered history. The literature itself, rarely distinguished for its methodological astuteness or sensitivity to problems of cohort inference, has predictably followed a confused and meandering course. More than a decade ago, an influential cohort analysis (Crittenden, 1962) based on a considerably broader time interval than had been available to us for *The American Voter* purported to show that the aging-conservatism hypothesis was in fact the true dynamic generator of the static relationship between age and the *direction* component of party identification, contrary to our original surmises.[3] This judgment stood as the "last word" in the literature for almost all of the 1960s. But after an unduly long lapse, the Crittenden demonstration was challenged, most notably by Cutler (1970), who pointed out a number of basic inadequacies in the cohort inferences involved. Still more recently, thanks in no small part to the more sophisticated work of Glenn and Hefner (1972) profiting from a still wider time frame, there has been a restoration of the conclusion, now apparently become quite consensual, that at least for this general period, the relationship between age and party identification has in fact been chiefly a generational rather than a life-cycle matter, exactly as we had originally conjectured.

At the same time, with scholarly attention swinging back the strength component, the literature seems destined for another agonizing period of misconstruction. In the past four years I have seen at least a half-dozen independently-generated cohort analyses of identification strength. Only one of these papers (Knoke and Hout, 1974), has claimed to find any sign of the predicted life-cycle gains in partisan intensity. All of the others, including some of the most recent, agree that such predicted gains cannot be found even when cohorts are traced over what is by now a very substantial span of time. Glenn (1972: 508), working with Gallup data, reviews our life-cycle interpretation of the age-strength relationship and concludes that his data "fail to provide any convincing evident of decreases in independence as a consequence of aging."[4] More recently, Abramson (1976) covers much of the same ground using the SRC-CPS (Survey Research Center-Center for Political Studies) election surveys, 1952-1974, and similarly judges that "there is no evidence that life-cycle effects account for the weak party loyalties of young Americans" (p. 478).[5] Both Glenn and Abramson, on the basis of their failure to find the predicted age-gain effects, come to the view that the static age-strength correlation visible throughout the period must thereby be a product of generational differences between cohorts. With the sole exception mentioned, all the other manuscripts follow suit. Hence the answer seems well on its way to a strong scholarly consensus.

My first order of business in this book will be to argue that with one nontrivial caveat, this conclusion is exactly wrong. Worse still, it is rooted in a simple logical impossibility, given other features of these cohort data about which all investigators are agreed. It will first be necessary to spend some time on an empirical analysis designed to show that the real world did not somehow heave forth such a logical impossibility. These demonstrations will not be very illuminating for those who understand the cohort problem since under the assumptions which I share with all others who have investigated the problem, there is no other way the data could fall. However, the fact that they fall the way they do brings some credibility to everyone's initial assumptions and thereby may make some contribution. Moreover, once we have covered this necessary ground, we shall explore our party identification cohort data in other directions as well.

I offer the contentious portions of this book in part because of my interest in the substance of the matter itself, and I hope that the period of muddling and confusion over the nature of the strength component will be more abbreviated than the corresponding period where the direction component was concerned.

I also offer them, however, in the belief that cohort analysis is an enormously important tool for social inquiry, which is deservedly coming into its own as survey research data on an increasing number of topics can boast of more and more extended time series, and hence rapid increases in their inferential possibilities. I consider it reasonable to suppose that cohort analysis as a technique is only at the dawn of its sophistication, a view that the rather clumsy exercises with party identification of the past fifteen years would seem to document. And while I have no ready-made or all-purpose codifications of the cohort analysis problem to suggest in ensuing pages, I hope that some of our critiques of earlier cohort work on party identification, which turn out to be quite varied in their texture and conceptual status, may help subsequent scholars working in related areas to avoid common pitfalls in the future.

The Methodological Side of the Problem

Some of the more recalcitrant difficulties in forming cohort inferences have only been sifted into plain view within the past ten years, although within that period the relevant literature has proliferated. I shall make no effort here to provide a well-rounded summary of these problems, since a number of excellent sources expressly devoted to such a task, or parts thereof, are available and especially if read end to end, provide quite suitable coverage.[6]

However, numerous of my later arguments would be quite obscure save in the light of several essential points to be made at the outset. Perhaps the most important of these points is that from a technical or "strict constructionist" point of view, cohort inferences in the general case are impossible. By such a strict point of view, I mean one which only accepts as hard evidence an unequivocal message locked up in a matrix of cohort data, and eschews the loose morals of a Parson Bayes in attending to side information or a priori grounds of plausibility. Within such an ascetic perspective, cohort inferences are intrinsically indeterminate.

This observation is not the most encouraging preface that might be found for the cohort analysis to follow, but it is sadly a necessary one. It is obvious that I intend in the long run to subvert the morals of my readers, or I should not be writing at all. Hence it is important to understand the indeterminacy problem, as well as my own posture toward it, if only to keep clear how and why the morals will be lost.

It is not at all hard to see intuitively why it is true, that if an investigator disposes of no more than one study at a single point in time, there is no strictly empirical basis for demonstrating that an observed relationship between age and some dependent variable of interest is of either the generational or the life-cycle type. There are two effects to be discriminated, but only a single diagnostic variable—age—with which to work. Age interpreted as generation (indexed by birth date) is perfectly correlated with chronological age (indexing a point in the life cycle) for all observations at such a single point in time. Technically, then, the problem is indeterminate, and any interpretation of such a static relationship in dynamic terms must depend entirely upon side information and appeals to plausibility tailored to the substance at hand.

If, however, the investigator has cross-sectional trend data covering longer and longer periods of time, with all relevant ages represented at each time point, this fact alone should ensure that birth date and chronological age would become, as it were, increasingly "decorrelated," thereby providing the two variables necessary to distinguish the two sets of effects. It would then seem obvious that even the most rudimentary cohort analysis should be able to conclude whether the observed relationship with age is a life-cycle or generational matter. All one needs to do is to inspect whether cohorts over two distant time points show a movement from "younger" to "older" positions on the variable in question. If they do, we might conclude that the static relationship owes its life to maturational processes. If instead cohorts show no systematic signs of change with aging, then we must return to the hypothesis of historical generations to account for observed cohort differences.

In some important special cases, cohort analysis is every bit as straightforward as this account implies. But the general case is at least one step more complex. Our example presumed that the true interpretation involved *either* one of these effects or the other, and not complex mixtures of the two; and it assumed as well that the basic parameters of any life-cycle effects would remain recognizably constant over the full period of observation. Still more important, it presumed that there were only two classes of effects, whereas it can be argued with merit that there are in fact three, or at the very least, a good two-and-a-half.

The third factor arises because the "generational" rubric can easily be subdivided into two more or less distinct classes of effects. The more classic "generation" effect inherited from studies in biology or demography involves variables which are in some relatively permanent sense "imprinted" —either through genetic dictates or socialization processes— upon the units of observation before they enter the investigator's field of view. The values with which varying cohorts enter the field of view differ as a function of their generation or birth date, but the "imprint" can be taken to have constant effects for the remainder of the lifetime. This need not mean that each cohort, once given its characteristic imprint, cannot change in its observed values on the dependent variable at later stages, although this would go beyond the classic "generational" effect in pure form. Perhaps some life-cycle variation is overlaid upon the characteristic value for the cohort upon entry, and the cohorts do indeed show internal variation over time. The important point is that cohorts do have characteristically different entering values, and whatever subsequent life trajectory is displayed is correspondingly incremented or decremented, according to the (relatively) high or low point of departure of that cohort.

But many attributes—in fact, most which readers of this book are likely to find interesting—are subject to further dynamic mutations in response to historic events during the full life span of the persons under study. While such adult changes clearly can be placed quite appropriately under the "generational" rubric, they are worth distinguishing from the classic generational effects as earlier described. Often they are called "period effects," with the "generational" label reserved for the constant-imprint case, a usage which we shall also adopt.

One particularly diabolical implication of such period effects, where relevant, is that there is often no a priori ground for assuming that their impacts on our units of observation are at all constant or simple across ages. Perhaps the same historical configuration which depresses values of the dependent variable among forty-year-olds is, if the truth were known, increasing the values of the same dependent variable among fifty-year-olds, is having no effect for sixty-year-olds, and is a depressant again after the age of seventy. And if this sounds too neatly geared to the life cycle, it is easy to imagine that the flow of events a year or two later may be playing upon the adult population with a totally different configuration of impacts. Similarly, one can arrive at still more complex but logically possible models in which current period effects stand in nonobvious interactive relationships with varying levels (high, medium or low, for example) of the pure-generational starting-point, as well as the current chronological age.

Indeed, in the general case, Pandora's box is opened wide. And with three such classes of effects permitted, but only two diagnostic variables, the problem is as a formal matter underidentified, and hence intrinsically indeterminate, at least within the immediate terms of conventional proof through the manipulation of numerical matrices of cohort values, however long the time span of observation may be. In a superficial way, there are three measured variables in long-term cohort data: period of the study; years of age; and date of birth. But as Mason et al. (1973) point out, each is completely defined in terms of the other two.

If all this be true, and cohort inference in the general case is impossible, how then are convincing cohort inferences ever made at all as they seem to be from time to time? Technically, they appear to depend on plausibility hinged on side information about the phenomenon at hand, and occasionally, on considerations of parsimony. What the side information typically does, again technically, is to permit the investigator to assume, at a level of greater or lesser plausibility, that one of the competing effects can be set to zero or at the very least that its peculiar impact can be prespecified on other grounds, so that it can be artificially removed from the nexus, leaving two unknown effects and two diagnostic variables. As in any such game, how compelling the final inferences may be to the scientific community depends largely on the plausibility of the constraining assumptions.

Types of Side Information. Since it is by way of side information and plausibility demonstrations that I intend to subvert the morals of the reader, the subject bears more direct discussion. To pick a frequently-cited kind of instance, let us imagine that we are about to perform a cohort analysis involving literacy rates, and are dealing with various national populations of adults over the age of twenty. Now highly reliable side information tells us (1) that many adults have learned to read after age twenty, over the sweep of historical time; but that (2) in most (not all) current populations these instances are rare and represent no more than a chemical trace in such populations. Hence, vis-à-vis this vast majority of populations, while period effects cannot strictly speaking be set at zero, they could be expected to approach zero so closely that no reasonably gross conclusions of other sorts would tend to be affected by the difference. In such instances, other cohort inferences would be extremely straightforward, and given the manifest plausibility of the assumptions, such inferences would be quite compelling. However, we also know that some mobilizing governments in underdeveloped countries have mounted massive and at least fairly successful adult literacy campaigns. (This is again pure and simple side information, which anybody immersed in a literacy study might be expected to have.) If such a population were blindly included, and its presumed period effects set to zero, the cohort inferences for that country would undoubtedly lose at least some degree of credibility. On the other hand, another piece of available side information would involve the more precise period in which such a campaign was taking place, and it might well be feasible to set period effects to zero only outside such a known span of time, thereby restoring credibility to the inferences. Throughout, side information determines what assumptions are plausible and, in the normal way, how compelling the conclusions may be taken to be.

Where the party identification variable is concerned, it is obvious that our side information is less incisive than in the literacy illustration. On the other hand, it is scarcely as though we are bereft of any such side information whatever, and we certainly enjoy a richer treasury of such information than would be the case were we setting out to study, for example, attitudes toward professional sports. We would propose, among other things, to keep such side information in mind.

We shall pay particular attention in the party identification case to the kind of side information that emerges directly from the configuration of the cohort data in themselves, rather than other peculiarities of the case, such as what the Republican Party leadership did in the 1970-1974 period and the like. The latter type of information is certainly fair evidence as side information, if relevant. But in attending to insights to be drawn from the data configuration in itself, we hope to highlight a kind of side information which may be helpful to other scholars attempting cohort analyses with other subject matters.

Let us present a loose example or two, with others to follow in the course of our empirical analysis. While no configuration of cohort data can in the general case be reduced to a unique generating mechanism or mechanisms, this fact should hardly be taken to mean that any such configuration is compatible with all plausible generating mechanisms. It is likely to be strictly incompatible with at least some plausible explanatory mechanisms, which may thereby be ruled out. In the ideal case, where only one of the more plausible generating mechanisms cannot be ruled out, we certainly have made a good deal of progress, even though there will always remain one or more implausible competitors which cannot, save for their implausibility, be definitively excluded. In less ideal cases, being able to rule out any plausible rival hypotheses shifts some increase in precious plausibility to the remainder. Sometimes the pattern of definitive exclusions itself provides a kind of side information which renders certain members of the remaining set more plausible than they may have been before the data were examined.

A second example is of a different texture, although it again refers to convenient side information often available even in the general case. The now-classic explanation for the indeterminacy of cohort inference is, as we have seen, that there are three classes of effects, but only two diagnostic variables, even with cross-time cohort data. This formulation is neat to the point of epigram, and is pedagogically a very useful one. But we shall discover that its meaning frays badly as our detailed cohort analyses proceed. In particular, we shall find that the two historical classes of effect (generation and period), however clear they may seem conceptually, blur badly in practice; and that what gets accounted as "two classes of effects" may often represent what may profitably be seen as no more than a single "variable." Sad to say, they may also represent in the same sense many more than even two such "variables."

Let us postpone the more complex case for much later in our inquiry. The case in which the two historical effects may boil down, for practical purposes, into a single variable is one in which the same historical conjuncture which is depressing or stimulating the attribute of adults already in the population being studied is having parallel effects on younger members not yet in the investigator's field of view. This means that as these younger members do emerge into the population being studied, they may well enter with values characteristically different from those cohorts which had entered before the historical impact registered. Thus technically these differences represent "generation effects," rather than the "period effects" displayed by their elders, in terms of our initial definitions. But in this instance, of course, the distinction is by construction a totally artificial one, depending as it does on the happenstance of research design (the minimal age for inclusion in the population under study) rather than any substantive matter. And a distinction as artificial as this is surely not strong enough to sustain the count of a full *three* unknowns in the initial epigram, although technically some further true generational effect may remain present.

Now in a slightly more complex case the same historical impact may register differently upon those within the investigator's field of view and those as yet too young to have entered it. The amplitude of response may differ, as may the permanence of the imprint. In some rare cases even the presence or the direction of the response might be entirely disjunctive, just at the boundary which the investigator has chosen to define his field of view. In such rare cases, there is very likely to be side information about the substance at hand to suggest explicitly that this may be so. But in lieu of any positive information to the contrary, all plausibility would seem to lie with an expectation that there would be a considerable continuity of effects across the age boundary limiting the field of view. In other words, for an "adult" study starting with twenty-one-year-olds, it would seem more rather than less plausible to imagine that whatever seeming "period effects" were registering on those twenty-one and twenty-two were probably having somewhat parallel influence on those nineteen and twenty at the same point in historical time. Thus a generating model that postulated totally different "period" and "generation" effects to account on the one hand for those just over twenty-one and on the other for those soon to become twenty-one would be intrinsically less compelling than a simpler model which, if it envisioned two different historical effects at all, at least left them continuous or interdependent in some sense. It is for this reason that we noted earlier, a bit facetiously, that the two classes of historical effects might be no more than one-and-a-half.

The important point for our immediate purposes is the likelihood that the cohort data configuration itself contains clues (such as later entry values displaced in degree and direction like changes wrought by recent period effects) which simplify the problem and render certain diagnoses far more plausible than others, even though proof positive may still be missing.

The Role of Parsimony. One of the more hallowed criteria for selection between rival hypotheses is parsimony. I have some reservations about such a ranking, and normally tend to agree with some of the suggestions of Gregg and Simon (1967) concerning the ease with which the importance of parsimony can be exaggerated. I would prefer to see parsimony left as a tie-breaker of last resort, when all else has failed.

Yet the very indeterminacy of cohort analysis means that we shall have this need for an ultimate tie-breaker far more often than usual, and I shall quite unabashedly turn to parsimony as a point of arbitration. I shall consider relative parsimony as contributing to an increase in relative plausi-bility whenever the occasion warrants. I doubt that my understandings as to what constitutes relative parsimony in this setting are at all unconventional. If all the contours of a particular batch of cohort data can be neatly understood within the terms of a single class of effects (with the other two possible effects implicitly set to zero), I shall prefer it to other models which may account for the data equally well in a mathematical sense, but which draw two or all three factors into (nonzero) motion. I shall consider common linear and log-linear additive models involving multiple effects to be preferable, ceteris paribus, to competing models requiring more complex interactions.[7] I shall assume that unless the cohort data themselves speak loudly to the contrary, para-meters of relevant dynamic processes tend to remain con-stant, at least to a reasonable approximation, over the intermediate term.

None of these assumptions estrange me at all from other cohort analysts of party identification. Indeed, the majority of them operate under an implicit assumption that cohort inference is a single-factor matter, and that the game is merely to decide that an age relationship is due to either life-cycle impacts or historical causes. While I am thoroughly delighted when I can arrive at such judgments myself, I will hope to remain with the minority of cohort analysts who maintain sensitivity to more complex possibilities and keep an eye out for situations in which their introduction is necessitated by the data. And while I shall respect and employ parsimony as a tie-breaking criterion, I would be unlikely to do so where a slightly more complex model enjoyed more support from relevant side information than a simpler competitor.

NOTES

1. The nature of the relationship between age and partisanship attracted the attention of the Lazarsfeld group at Columbia and the early election studies of the University of Michigan series, and produced a widely cited article by Crittenden (1962). A representative, although by no means exhaustive, list of some of the more recent and most explicit cohort-analytic discussions of the subject might include Cutler (1970), Glenn and Hefner (1972), Glenn (1972), Knoke and Hout (1974), Nie, Verba and Petrocik (1976), and Abramson (1976).

2. While these expectations have been shown to have merit in a half-dozen to a dozen countries for which data are available, they have failed to be confirmed in some few others. Clearly there are other local conditions, including such recalcitrant ones as political ethos or culture where parties and voting are concerned, that intrude upon the dynamics suggested here.

3. Crittenden, working with the Gallup partisanship item which lacks any probe as to strength of partisanship, did not attempt to address the strength component.

4. Glenn tried to leave his conclusions tentative, particularly as he lacked any actual strength measurement for the Gallup partisanship variable. However, the finding has been seized upon by Abramson and others as rather more definitive.

5. Actually, the particular Abramson analysis is limited to whites.

6. Good as openers are Riley (1973) and Mason et al. (1973). See also Schaie (1965), Baltes (1968) and Cohn (1972).

7. We add the log-linear term deliberately, because we are dealing in a domain where exponential functions of the passage of time are common. They seem to me obviously to be expected in this setting, and we shall not take them to be significantly more strange or complex than linear relationships.

Chapter 2

SOME FIRST PROBES OF THE
STRENGTH COMPONENT

With all of these conceptual considerations in mind, we may now turn to a reanalysis of the cross-time behavior of the strength component of party identification. Since the basic cohort data file I shall use diverges in greater or lesser degree from those used by others in published reports, it is useful to review its origin and current scope.

In 1957, as background work for the cohort-analysis verdicts to be passed concerning party identification in *The American Voter,* I established an open-ended file of data on party identification organized by annual cohorts, drawing from every source which seemed relevant. It will be recalled that the first measure of the party identification variable in its now classic form was conducted in connection with the Survey Research Center 1952 Election Study. This meant that the time base for even crude cohort guesses was precariously narrow, and the case numbers available from the

1952, 1954 and 1956 election studies were precariously thin. Therefore I added to the file three national surveys from other SRC programs which had asked the party identification item. As time span was even more critical than case numbers, 1958 data which became available in 1959 between manuscript and press were checked against our tentative verdicts and folded into the file. I also went through the considerable labor of converting the 1944 NORC election study, which had an item similar to the party identification item, into as comparable a sample and measurement as possible in order to provide at least one reference point more remote in time. I did not include Gallup materials, both out of a distrust of the sampling methods and because the most nearly-relevant Gallup item had no explicit measure of the strength component. These materials were the basis for our final 1960 verdicts on the matter.[1]

The file was constructed in open-ended fashion because it was obvious that increasing time spans of the same cohort data would be of vital interest. And indeed, over ensuing years I have kept the file reasonably well updated, plugging in the results from each new SRC or CPS study as it has become available. Because of occasional lapses of attention on my part, I cannot guarantee that the file contains every Survey Research Center sample bearing on party identification, although it surely approaches that status: it is most probably complete, and is certainly not missing more than one or two studies.[2]

As of this writing, the file includes some twenty-nine adult national sample studies conducted by the Survey Research Center between 1952 and 1975, in which over 40,000 individual respondents figure and have been organized by birth year and chronological age. The file is thus well over double the size of Abramson's (1976) SRC file covering nearly the same period. It contains more discrete samples for the 1952-1975 period than the central data reported from Glenn's (1972) Gallup file for the 1945-1971 period, although only about two-thirds as many individual cases.

Owing to the peculiar evolution of this file, as chronicled above, it has certain peculiarities, which are catalogued in summary form as Appendix A of this book. It may reassure the reader, however, to know that as best I can tell, none of the divergences in conclusions from the growing consensus about age gains are a function of differences in the data bases used. I have put the data from my file into forms replicating those presented by Glenn, Abramson and others as a specific check on this matter. In each case, while there are naturally a myriad of differences in specific numbers (at the second or third-digit level), the gross contours of the data seem essentially indiscriminable in all respects important for the debate. In short, I am convinced that the difference in raw data base accounts for none of our differences in interpretation; and that if Glenn, Abramson or the other cohort analysts had approached my file with their own procedures and conceptions of cohort analysis, they would have been led to the Glenn-Abramson conclusions.

Conventional Searches for Age Gains. What are the procedures normally used in searching for the predicted age gains in identification strength? Save for Knoke and Hout, they are very much of the same cloth, although the precision of the "test" varies, and at first blush they appear to be utterly straightforward. One divides the data into cohorts of one or another width, and then enters appropriate means or proportions indexing party identification strength across the sequence of observations from the start of the file to its end, i.e., while the cohort is held constant but is "aging." One does this for all cohorts of reasonable length and case numbers.

Variation in precision of the "test" is roughly as follows: In the loosest cases, the investigator presents the basic cohort matrix, and invites the reader to scan across rows to see for himself whether there is any sense of reliable upward progression in the entries. Typically there is not, and the case is considered clinched. More quantitatively oriented papers take stock of the numbers of cohorts that can be seen to have made net gains in strength over the period of observation, as opposed to those registering net losses. This more precise test is easily implemented by subtracting the terminal value for each cohort from its first observed value, a process which I shall call for convenience the "endpoint method." Then the balance sheet is dressed, and although I have seen several such balances independently constructed, I do not recall so much as one in which the number of cohorts showing net gains diverged from the number showing losses by more than two, and most have shown a tie or but one cohort difference. Typical scores are 8-6, 6-6, 7-6 and so on. One does not have to have much statistical sophistication to know that these empirical contrasts are pretty thin gruel, and that it would be foolhardy to reject the null hypothesis of "no age gains." So the null verdict is accepted although, as we shall see, the investigator has thereby fallen into a classic instance of a Type II error: failure to reject the null hypothesis when in fact it is false.

The Basic Parameters of the Special Case. We shall let the fatal weaknesses of the "endpoint method" in this special case sift to light one by one as we proceed with our own diagnosis of the situation. But before we plunge into the confusing details of counting tree rings, it makes sense first to survey the gross contours of the forest about to be explored.

There are in fact two prime features of the special case before us. The first serves to pose the question, while the second goes a long way toward answering it (if not, strictly speaking, all the way). Happily, neither of these empirical features of the situation seems subject to any controversy. Glenn (1972: 508) sums them up as the central features in so many words, and no other investigator leaves any doubt as to his complete awareness of them.

The first feature is the abiding positive relationship between the strength component and chronological age in all static, cross-section samples taken individually within the

United States from the present back to 1952 for SRC data; back to 1945 for Glenn's Gallup data; and it shows through clearly even in the NORC 1944 data.[3] The magnitude of the correlation is not deafening, by comparison with more exact sciences; but against the normal run of nonexperimental correlations attracting comment in the looser disciplines, it would have to rank as "strong." Furthermore, if we examine even the gross data more closely, we might profitably note (as others have noted) that while the magnitude of that correlation does not appear to vary beyond sampling error throughout the period from 1944 to 1964, it begins to increase steeply as of 1966 and beyond.

This persistent static correlation is, of course, what defines our problem: we introduce cohort analysis in an effort to decide which of several plausible rival generating mechanisms are responsible for the shape it assumes in static data.

Several broad hints as to a likely answer are imbedded in the cross-time behavior of the strength component at the total aggregate level over the thirty-year period available for observation. Figure 1 presents this tableau as drawn from our own SRC data file; Glenn's Gallup data, while varying somewhat in finer detail, duplicates the main features of interest to us quite nicely.[4]

Most notably Figure 1 suggests about as clearly as such a graph could that the full thirty-year period divides itself into two distinct subperiods. For most of the span, the aggregate level of identification strength appears to have been, within expectable sampling error at least, a simple constant of the American scene. Between 1964 and 1966, however, it begins a brusque descent; and the smoothness and ultimate depth of this descent is thoroughly striking, continuing as it does over all the final third of the total period. The visual impression of two distinct subperiods is striking enough, although it is underscored by some simple regression calculations formed on the SRC-CPS trend data, relating change in aggregate identification strength to the passage of real time:

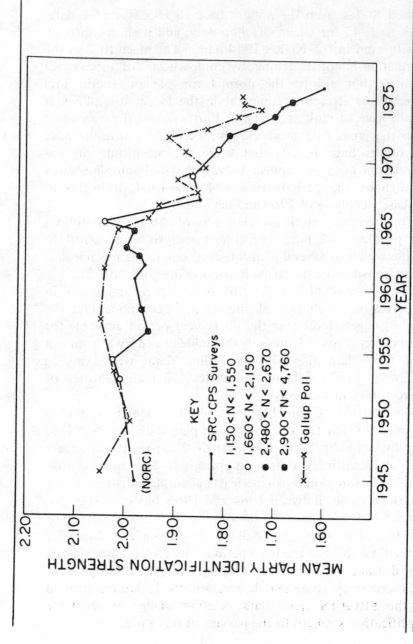

Figure 1: AGGREGATE LEVELS OF PARTY IDENTIFICATION STRENGTH IN THE NATIONAL ELECTORATE, 1944-1975

	r	b Change per annum	N
1952 to February, 1965	+ .013	+ .000 (09)	10
February, 1965 to 1975	− .962	− .034	10

Furthermore, it should not be forgotten that this temporally-discrepant behavior of the mean strength term over this period is entirely reminiscent of the magnitudes of the static age-strength correlations, which were similarly constant up to 1966 and then began to rise progressively, although these two empirical facts are not mathematically-necessary concomitants.

These are the broadest parameters of our special case that seemed important to highlight. We have not as yet looked at a single disaggregated cohort, but it might behoove us to stop and ponder these parameters a moment, particularly in combination, if only as a guide to desirable cohort analysis tactics to apply in this special case.

If we recall the treacheries of cohort diagnosis outlined in the preceding section, we shall wish to proceed with consummate care. In particular, since we ultimately wish to assign weights (possibly including zeroes) to various dynamic processes generating the key static relationships, we will surely want to maximize our chances that the key parameters of those several processes are not shifting around under our feet during whatever period our cohort analyses cover. For such would add a whole new level of indeterminacy to a problem already near death in indeterminacy. Obviously, this is not an easy order, since the processes are hidden and are what we are trying to learn something about. However, in this special case, Figure 1 screams that the full thirty-year period is unlikely to have been homogeneous with respect to such underlying process parameters.[5]

Most of the period suggests a delicate equilibrium between whatever hidden generating mechanisms are operative, leaving the aggregate result constant. But this constancy is intruded upon, in 1966 and thereafter, by forces that look very much like "period effects." Indeed, we shall see later that what happens in the post-1966 period fits the classical definition of period effects to an uncanny perfection.

The main moral of all this for our cohort analysis plans is that we should not want to analyze the whole 1944-1974 period in one lump, as though it were homogeneous. Such a procedure will simply make a problem which is already formally intractable a complete shambles. Yet this is exactly what the "endpoint method" as employed by all save one of our predecessors is implicitly doing. It rests on two observations, one in the first subperiod, which we shall henceforth call the "steady-state period," and the other after the apparent intrusion—and with considerable force—of special period effects. Whether one's final endpoint is in 1968, or 1972, or 1974, the results are quite predictable. If the period effects were acting to increase the strength component, the age gains characteristic of the "steady-state period" would likely be highly overestimated. As it is, with the period effects depressing party identification strength, any age gains that may have characterized the earlier period are at least going to be underestimated by the end-point method, and may even become totally obscured, depending on the relative strengths of the competing forces involved.

Only Glenn, in his second paper on the subject, recognizes this problem and its practical import for the conduct of a cohort analysis.[6] He reasons very properly that the intrusion of period effects might well cashier any honest search for the elusive age gains. Therefore he does another search, restricting his attention to data from what we are calling the steady-state period.[7] Again, however, he finds no reliable sign of age gains in partisan strength, a result which means that his earlier verdicts favoring a generational interpretation of the static relationship over the life-cycle possibility are strongly reinforced; and which means for us that our current detective story still has several reels to run.

It is clear on the face of it that Glenn is dealing with a different variable, although a related one, and with a different data base, than any of the competing cohort analyses of the strength component which have confirmed his failure to find the age gains. In point of fact, we are not about to dismiss his findings on such grounds alone: there are several further problems with his treatment, and these could easily account for divergences in judgment quite apart from the lack of time or sampling comparability. However, the comparability problem must be addressed sooner or later in any event, so let us do so more or less parenthetically here.

The Gallup question is normally worded:

"In politics, as of today, do you consider yourself a Republican, Democrat, or Independent?"

The SRC party identification question is worded:

"Generally speaking, do you usually think of yourself as a Republican, Democrat, Independent, or what?"

This root item is followed with probes to ascertain the strength of the identification when such exists. The items appear almost identical to casual glance. However, the "generally" and "usually" qualifiers in the SRC question were originally intended to broaden the time reference and properly classify the long-term identifier who is momentarily piqued at his own party, or tempted to defect temporarily to vote for a charismatic candidate of another party. A verb like "consider" in the Gallup question has somewhat parallel, if perhaps weaker, overtones; but the "as of today" invites in the baldest way a very transient frame of reference.

I have done many casual comparisons of the two items in the past twenty years, and their similarities and divergences seem to be almost exactly what one might predict from such a face analysis alone. For most respondents most of the time, they are extremely likely to elicit the same choice of party. Surely in a static sense applied to the same samples they would show intercorrelations of .60 at the very least, and more likely something in the .80-.90 range. This means for very many crude purposes, the substantive results analyzed for the two wordings competitively would be very likely to show indistinguishable results. On the other hand, the face differences in content bear chiefly on the time referent, all of which might suggest that the maximal differences between the two items is likely to occur around problems involving temporal dynamics. It is my impression that this in fact happens: the Gallup item is visibly more volatile and situation-bound than the SRC party identification measure. The differences are neither enormous nor frightening, especially for work involving no more than crude approximations with the direction component. The SRC question swings but faintly, although more than we would like, in response to the immediate political tides; the Gallup question swings more, as best we can see from our very casual comparisons. It is almost as though respondents were paying attention to the details of wording of the two questions.

When we turn to the strength component, which is more relevant for us at the moment, the problems are manifestly more grave. The SRC item has an explicit strength measure, and the Gallup item does not. Indeed, I have been somewhat perplexed to find a large amount of work with an explicit strength measure challenged on the basis of an item which not only fails to have a perfectly comparable measure, but has never purported to have one at all. Once again, there is enough similarity between the initial threshold of the SRC item (party vs. independent) and the Gallup discrimination, issues of time referent aside, that the "two" strength components are surely correlated at a nontrivial level. But I would be surprised if the correlations were anything like as high as for the direction component; and where the further details of the two measurements are concerned, we are comparing something with nothing so that there is little else to be said.

It is likely that this discrepancy has at least some little bearing on Glenn's inability to find age gains in the strength component even during the steady-state period; and it is conceivable that it accounts for all of the difference. I tend to think not, however. If I have properly construed Glenn's procedures, I strongly suspect that even with data from our SRC file organized in this form, Glenn would have determined that no age gains are visible and hence that the effects have to be generational instead. In Glenn's form, they certainly look quite lifeless also.

We are nearing a moment when we can fruitfully begin our own cohort analysis of the strength component. We have learned, among other things, that if we want an outside chance of estimating competing cohort effects reliably, we must at the very least treat our thirty-year span as being comprised of two distinct periods in this special case. In fact we will follow the Glenn tactic quite directly, by limiting our first search for the elusive age gains to data from the steady-state period. The remainder of this chapter and the next are committed to this pursuit; only in the fourth chapter shall we turn to a consideration of the strength component, 1966 and beyond.

However, we are not entirely finished with lessons to be drawn from the gross contours of the data—the two major and noncontroversial features highlighted somewhat earlier. Let us consider the static age-strength relationship jointly with the long-term aggregate constancy in identification strength displayed over a full two decades from 1944 where the survey eye can first see (hence, quite conceivably, still earlier), on to some date like 1965. Let us add another unimpeachable empirical observation: during this period in the United States older persons tended to die out of the population at much faster rates than younger people. Like the first two empirical facts, this would seem thoroughly beyond dispute, and a matter central to the thinking of all of our cohort analysts.

To these three indisputable facts, let us add one somewhat softer but heuristic assumption, which we can treat as provisional. This is the assumption that we are dealing with a simple cohort effect, rather than some diabolically complex configuration of all or most effects at once. I must insist once again that the addition of this disputable assumption does not in any sense depart from the preconceptions of any of my predecessor cohort analysts. Only Glenn's later work even seems to countenance the possibility of complex effects, although they do not figure in his most relevant substantive verdicts; and the others proceed on a "gotta be this or that" assumption which differs in no way from the assumption I propose to add to our three root facts.

If we accept the joint implications of the three root facts and only wish to permit simple effects, then unless I am greatly mistaken, for the steady-state period the Glenn-Abramson verdict is in a strict sense a logical impossibility in accounting for the static age-strength relationship, and an age-gain, life-cycle verdict is a logical necessity!

The argument is straightforward. The generational effect espoused by Glenn, Abramson and others is of a classic sort, resting on the imprint of early socialization into greater or lesser party militance. The strong static age relationship with the strength component that is visible at the very outset of observation, in 1944 or 1945, is construed as existing because of these inter-cohort differences in earlier imprints. The old are strongly identified, because of their training. The young are notably less identified. Thus far, there is no way of contesting the assumption. But as we let the passage of time unwind, and the strongly-imprinted old die out at rapid rates and are replaced progressively by the weakly-imprinted young, the aggregate level of identification in the population *must* decline correspondingly, since the Glenn-Abramson verdict already has ruled out the internal cohort age gains which might shore it up. However, we are all agreed that one of the prime features of the empirical situation is that there was no change at all, much less a decline, in the aggregate levels of these identifications for the next twenty years. Hence as a logical system these three facts are incompatible with the verdict, under a simple-effects assumption. The age-gain, life-cycle interpretation is not only painlessly compatible with all three facts at once: if we only permit simple effects, it is the unique verdict possible.

It may seem ironic that we have arrived at such a flat cohort diagnosis about this special case, without even as yet dirtying our hands with a shred of disaggregated cohort data. It is indeed a special case, and we would scarcely argue that detailed cohort analyses are generally unnecessary. Quite the contrary. Even in our special case, there are soft spots and loopholes which only more detailed work can address. We have insisted to date, for example, on a simple-effects assumption; and the preceding chapter should warn us this is likely to be naive. Or again, perhaps the aggregate level of identifications *did* decline over the twenty-year steady-state but not sharply enough to be disentangled from sampling error. If this latter possibility were true, it would place us in a very trying situation indeed, because we shall never again, in descending to the disaggregate cohort level, be as free of sampling error (relatively) as when we first contemplate the full aggregate contours of our file. However this may be, there are a variety of ways to estimate relative magnitudes in order to ask more incisively whether sampling error could conceivably mask a decline in aggregate identification strength sufficient to account for the fact that static age-strength relationships looked at the end of the steady-state period just as they did at the beginning.

So we have only begun our work, but the important general lesson to draw from these preliminaries is that it is often well worthwhile to look at the forest before the trees where cohort analyses are concerned, as we have done here. Side information is crucial in this kind of effort, as we argued in the first chapter. And some of the best side information is scarcely outside at all: it can be drawn from gross features of the cohort data configuration itself, with a little common sense sprinkled in. It would rarely if ever be true that such a configuration would alone provide the definitive cohort diagnosis, if multiple or complex effects cannot be ruled out. But it can provide a good deal of precious guidance.

NOTES

1. From the above, it should be clear that Abramson's (1976) report that we precluded any tentative effort to evaluate cohort gains in party identification "by combining the results of surveys conducted at different times . . ." is simply not true. Presumably he refers to a central table (Campbell et al., 1960: 162) which does combine the data from the seven surveys of my file to display the relationship between chronological age and party identification strength. How-ever, the decision to organize the table in the form presented was simply one end-result of all of our more detailed cohort-analytic work. That is, since the data seemed to make clear that party identification was a function of chronological age and not of generational differences, it was legitimate to combine observation times to provide the most robust possible estimate of that chronological age relationship. Had our verdict been the opposite, it would have been necessary to organize any such time-collapsed table by birth year, not chronological age.

2. I was least attentive to this file in the latter half of the 1960s. In fact, I have only been able to devote analytic attention to it at three points since 1960. In the late 1960s, in response to graduate student queries as to why I was still teaching that the direction component was chiefly generational in spite of Crittenden's "proof" to the contrary, I did a sketchy reconnaissance of the direction component to make sure that his verdict was still wrong. I returned to the file in 1973 to look over the strength component out of comparable perplexity at Glenn's (1972) conclusions, and drafted all parts of this book bearing on reasons for divergent conclusions at that time. I have returned to round it off under the joint stimulus of a further wave of manuscript "confirmations" of Glenn's conclusions, without reference to Knoke and Hout's more appropriate findings; an unusually rich haul of party identification readings in 1974 field work; and a sabbatical leave.

3. It is also true, although not crucial to our argument here, that in a fair majority of other political systems the same static relationship is observable, and some of the few exceptions can be readily predicted from the core theory concerning these processes (Converse, 1969).

4. Detailed explanation for the mode of calculating the values presented in Figure 1 are provided in Appendix B.

5. I am tempted to say that Figure 1 rules out such a possibility at the most pristine mathematical level. I shall refrain from committing myself to such a

statement, since I have not taken the parlor-game time to push numbers around in order to see whether any configuration of such parameters could exist which, while themselves remaining constant, could generate the time trace of Figure 1. Certainly the reader will understand that all plausibility (in a looser sense) rides with the two-period assumption.

6. Abramson (1976) reports that W. Phillips Shively brought this problem to his attention between an early draft and the final version of his manuscript, as well as another point which will figure strongly in our argument later. Abramson does not take strong issue with such a correction; but neither does he appear to feel that it negates his conclusions that generational factors, and not life-cycle age gains, have been the main generator of the age-strength relationship over the 1952-1974 period.

7. There is a minor divergence between us here as to the dating of the steady-state period. For reasons that are quite intelligible, Glenn is somewhat vague about his dating. He is dealing with Gallup studies lumped into gross time blocs, centered on and identified with crucial dates like 1957, 1961 and 1965 (for the period in question). At one point he describes the "1957" observations as the terminal ones for the constant period, and his most intensive search for age gains is within the 1945-1957 period. This might be taken to imply that the "steady-state" period had already ended before the turn of the decade. At another point he identifies the turning point by implication as the outset of the 1960s; at still another, not until 1965. The reason for the vagueness is simply that his Gallup data show the lumped "1961" observations to display a slight downturn in proportion independent, relative to the 1957 reading. But it is only the next reading, in "1965," that shows any serious downturn. Therefore it is a moot point whether the first real intrusion of these period effects is to be dated as early as 1958, or as late as 1965. The SRC data in Figure 1 are considerably less equivocal in this regard. There is no sign of any parallel sag early in the 1960s; and the downward trend begins crisply between the 1964 and 1966 studies, coincident with the first noteworthy Gallup decline. We shall therefore identify the termination of the "steady state" as lying between 1964 and 1966, for purposes of this book.

Chapter 3

ON FINDING THE VERY SMALL

In addition to the difficulties already discussed in the preceding chapter, there are a number of other defects in prior cohort analyses carried out by loose inspection or by the "endpoint method," which virtually assure that age gains in party identification, that we now have seen are virtually a logical necessity for the steady-state period (1944-1964), will not be found. These defects are somewhat various, but many of them can be summarized as arising because the investigators have not stopped to ask about the nature of the effects they are trying to track down. They seem oblivious to magnitude expectations for the age gains, or where they should or should not expect such gains to occur. Hence the fact that their search is futile is not surprising.

Having agreed to focus our efforts on the steady-state period, let us ask just what it is we are looking for in these data. If we return to the theory underlying these matters, we

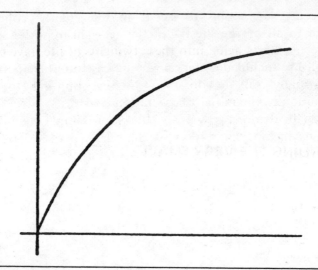

Figure 2: **PROTOTYPIC GAINS IN PARTY IDENTIFICATION STRENGTH AS A FUNCTION OF AGING**

may profitably note that the pure life-cycle effect, as hypothesized, involves gains in partisan strength that themselves progressively decrease in size over the life span. Such a negatively-accelerating function, as shown in Figure 2, signifies that age gains are likely to be much clearer in the early portions of adulthood than they are later on.

As an empirical matter, what happens among the elderly seems to vary somewhat from country to country. In some instances there is an actual decline of identification strength among the very old (e.g., after seventy years of age). In these cases the trajectory of the strength function over the life span fits very nicely what is known of the trajectory of political engagement or involvement, with its absolute decline in the latest stages of life, when the elderly shrink their attention to the microcosm and their immediate needs. In other instances, such as the United States, the static age relationship with the strength component merely seems to flatten out in the later years, rather than show any incisive decline.[1]

In neither of these instances, of course, is there any point in expecting age gains to occur in the elderly cohorts, although in all of the "tests" of the age-gain hypothesis we have seen, cohorts aging into these twilights of life have been mechanically included as far as waning case numbers permit, and naturally fail to do their bit in counting toward confirmation of the initial "expectation."

We shall demonstrate later that for simple technical reasons having nothing to do with the theory per se, there are also no clear expectations for cohorts that first come into view at the youngest ages, although these are often the cohorts that are included as the most crucial in such "tests."

By far the most basic problem in all of these prior cohort analyses of party identification, however, is a lack of any realistic conception either as to the magnitude of the age gains being sought or, more particularly, their relationship to the inevitable and pervasive "noise" level created by garden-variety sampling error. Such error is a constant problem in working around disaggregated cohort data, even from the very large samples now available to us, as we shall see both in this chapter and the next. It is natural in a dynamic context to want to keep time divided as finely as possible, both in the birth-year and the observation-period senses. Yet it is a constant battle, if one works finely at all, to maintain a discernible signal against the noise.

In the specific case at hand of age gains, there seems at first glance to be no problem. After all, the overall static relationship between age and partisan strength has always been quite imposing, and in recent years it has become absolutely stronger. On any national sample with at all conventional case numbers, there has never been any problem of confusing the static age-strength relationship with sampling error.

However, we would do well to remember that this total static relationship involves something on the order of a fifty- to sixty-year accumulation of partisan strength, whereas we can only follow specific cohorts for a very limited fraction of that period—in fact, for only twelve years in the SRC data, if we refrain from taking data outside the steady-state period. In other words, however imposing the overall age gains may be, we can only hope to find a quarter or a fifth of that total effect in the data available to us. All of which ensures us that any proper test of the age-gain expectation is condemned from the very outset to be looking for some rather tiny differences, just at the awkward moment when we begin to divide our large samples into finer cohorts, thereby radically increasing the level of noise from sampling error.

In short, it will be quite like hunting for a needle in the disheveled haystack of sampling error. If along with prior analysts we fail to assess in advance that the problem is of this character, then we are quite likely to assume that something large should jump out at us from the haystack. And when, after a cursory glance or two, nothing does, we will erroneously conclude that nothing is there, despite the fact that we have not seriously looked.

ESTIMATING EXPECTED AGE GAINS

What is the most rational way of determining just what effects we are looking for? The answer to this question seems self-evident. We know that age is not exactly the variable we should be working with, but only a rough surrogate. We also know that the magnitude of expected gain will vary somewhat according to the absolute age span being covered in longitudinal analyses of specific cohorts. Coupling these problems, our best estimate of expected effects should be drawn from the static relationship between age and partisan strength, as it has been observed during the steady-state period from 1952 to 1964, before it became in the most obvious way confounded by period effects.

The main curve plotted in Figure 3 shows this static relationship compounded from fourteen studies conducted by the Survey Research Center within the 1952-1964 period. Given the nearly 20,000 cases involved, we have felt that it is of some value to construct this plot on an annual basis, rather than using the most customary gross eight or ten-year cohort "widths." However, as one hedge against the noise of sampling error we have based these estimates of annual values on three-year moving averages. In other words, the strength value shown for persons age forty-eight is really based on the number of persons, about three times as numerous, who are ages forty-seven through forty-nine. The values for persons age forty-nine is similarly compounded of those forty-eight through fifty, and so on. This simple device is a very useful way of dealing with fine cohorts, while suppressing some of the wilder raggedness that sampling error would lay upon data based purely on cohorts a single year "wide."

Several observations need to be made about the main curve in Figure 3. First, we may note that this function does appear to be slightly nonlinear, in the theoretically expected direction of a deceleration in gains as age advances. The departure from linearity is not very impressive, and is undoubtedly less than our underlying theory would call for. However, we should remember that our theory is developed in terms of a predictor variable which is the length of time that a person has felt some psychological attachment to a particular party, rather than chronological age itself. Since Figure 3 uses age as an imperfect surrogate, such modest departures between observed and expected functions are not particularly distressing. And since our immediate purpose is to ask what gains in strength should be expected for various cohorts defined in terms of age, rather than the more incisive length-of-attachment variable, Figure 3 is admirably suited to our practical needs.

A second observation about the main curve in Figure 3 is that the prime irregularities present, relative to theoretical expectations, occur in the very earliest age cohorts. In general, below age twenty-six or so, the curve no longer plunges downward as one might extrapolate from the rest of the function. Inexplicable irregularities occur,[2] along with a

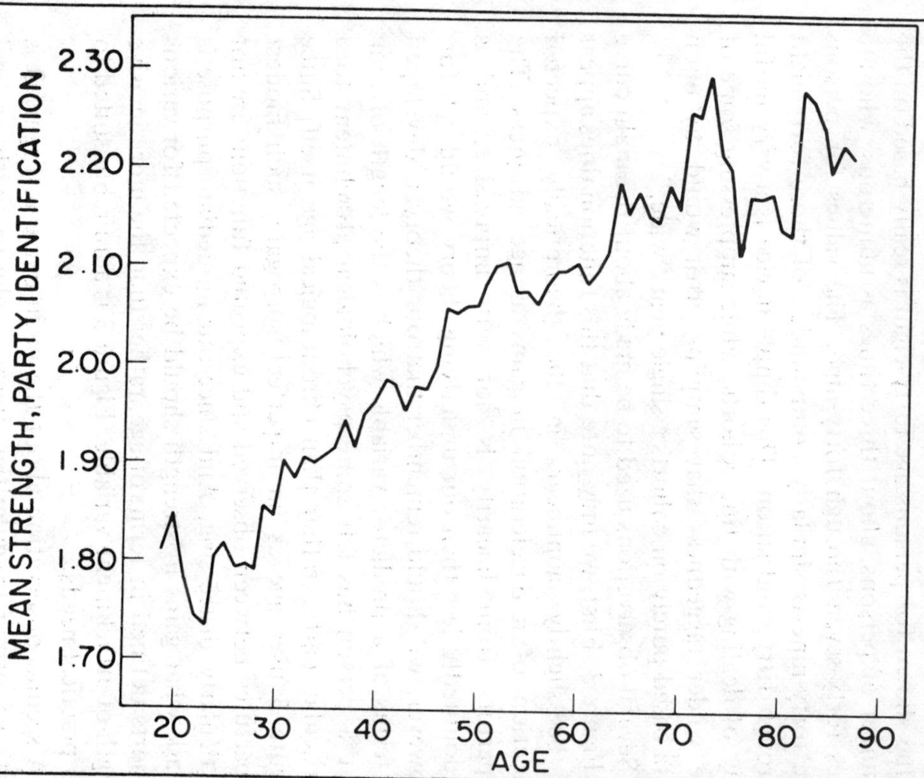

Figure 3: "STEADY-STATE" RELATIONSHIP, PARTY IDENTIFICATION STRENGTH BY AGE, 1952-1964

noteworthy upward "hook" in the youngest ages, a matter which has no interpretation in the parent theory.

We noticed this peculiar blemish initially nearly twenty years ago, when we first began to pyramid multiple samples by age. At first we took for granted that it was mere sampling error, since of course at that time our fine-cohort samples were dreadfully small. It persisted, however, as cohort case numbers built up. It is not visible in every single sample but in some it is accentuated, and Figure 2 naturally provides the best overall view of its appearance with large case numbers in hand. As time wore on, we became convinced it was "real," and we began to toy with theories involving the disjunction between childhood socialization and adult experience with the political world, in order to see if we could arrive at a clearer understanding of it.

We now have become convinced that this "hook" in the function reflects more an abiding technical difficulty of the sample survey operation than it does any interesting reality. It is well known that even the United States Census Bureau has great difficulty in locating young persons in their early twenties. This cohort is persistently and seriously under-enumerated, a fact which has been made plain historically by the re-emergence of this cohort in full strength in later enumerations of it in the age twenty-five through thirty range. Indeed, it has become common practive in constructing age tables of the population to "fudge" the data for this age range, dubbing in a suitable number of these temporarily-invisible citizens even though they have not been directly enumerated.[3]

It is not surprising that such a field problem is if anything compounded in routine survey operations whose sample designs hinge on more or less conventional dwelling units. That is, prisons, military installations and college dormitories are usually among the standard exemptions from such designs, which means that the young, or at least certain types of young, are likely to be missed at rates which even exceed the demonstrable and impressive underenumerations of the Census Bureau.

Indeed, it can be shown that Survey Research Center samples consistently underrepresent the cohorts of young people in the age twenty-one through twenty-four range by a dramatic 40-70 percent.[4] This severe underrepresentation evaporates with lightning speed over the ages of the twenties: for the cohort aged twenty-five through twenty-nine it is only a 7 percent decrement, and later age cohorts are quite accurately represented.

What is important, however, is that this entry cohort is enormously biassed away from young people who are transient, in the very Age of Transience. Ironically, it is this entry cohort, especially at the first observation period, which is dearest to the hearts of cohort analysts, and on which the greatest analytic weight is customarily placed. Yet when this initial cohort is "traced" over time for another five, ten or fifteen years, and most especially when an end-point comparison method is used, the investigator is committing willy-nilly one of the more heinous sins of cohort analysis: that of comparing incomparable populations. How disastrous the sin may be depends entirely on the degree to which the fact of youthful transience correlates with whatever dependent variable he may have under scrutiny.

In the special case of party identification strength, there are findings formed over total adult populations (not just the young) to suggest some relationship between community roots and stronger party identifications. There are also findings among the young to suggest lower political interest among the more transient (other better explanatory variables *not* controlled), and there is a modest but reliable relationship between political interest and strength of partisan identification.

We cannot say with any high level of confidence that the "hook" in the function portrayed in Figure 3 derives totally from this sampling bias.[5] But we can say that whatever bias exists for this first cohort—known to be substantial—would tend to have the effect of overestimating the strength of party identification in the initial cohort. Therefore the path of discretion would seem to require setting this first precious cohort aside, in any serious search for the elusive age gains. It can only obscure them, even though this is precisely the part of the life cycle when the gains should be most vigorous. Fortunately, the technical problem has largely, if not completely, disappeared after the age of twenty-five years or so.

With all of these considerations in mind, we are now ready to use the data from the curve in Figure 3 for estimating the magnitude of age gains to be expected of individual cohorts if *all* of the static age relationship captured there were due to a simple life-cycle accumulation during the steady-state period. We also have seen reason to limit our attention within the total curve to the central range of cohorts, ages twenty-six to seventy, where any gains should be most clear and reliable.

Within that range of ages, the cumulated static age relationship is not far off linear.[6] If we ignore the modest nonlinearity, and extract from the grouped data (cohort means) by conventional least squares methods an overall gain slope of a linear sort for the whole twenty-six through seventy age range, we find that such a gain averages .0082 per annum in the scalar currency being used. Or, alternatively, we can capture somewhat more of the nonlinearity, while staying within the comforts of simple linear estimation, by dividing the twenty-six through seventy range expediently into two segments, thereby establishing two moderately different gain rates for the earlier and the later portions of the life cycle. In this format, we find an average gain or slope which is .0108 for the earlier segment (ages twenty-six through fifty-three), and a lesser .0056 for the later segment (ages fifty-two through seventy).[7]

On the face of it, any of these slopes is bound to appear tiny, without doubt because of the initial zeroes involved.

They would seem subjectively larger, of course, if we were to multiply these per-annum expectations by the number of years of the steady-state period available to us for cohort examination (a period of twelve years, for both the SRC data and the Gallup data as Glenn has handled the latter), and such a multiplication is entirely in order. However, we can only arrive at a proper appraisal of the magnitude of these numbers if we reinsert them into the context of the game against error that the cohort analyst is obliged to play.

Fortunately, all the necessary parameters of that game can be simply calculated, once we know what we are looking for. Let us imagine that we are seeking to confirm gains of this size with a twelve-year observation period in which to work. Let us assume furthermore that our analytic procedures are those familiar from the past literature. That is to say, we are going to pay primary attention to endpoints, and in particular, we shall ask whether the mean identification strength across a set of cohorts visible for the full observation period differs significantly (at the conventional .05 level) in the first "reading" from what it is in the terminal observation twelve years later. Let us assume, finally—since the way our "expecteds" were formed requires it—that we have defined the search a little more tightly than any of our predecessors, by recognizing that the inclusion of people who are either over seventy or under twenty-six will do nothing but obscure the problem further. Hence to be eligible for the "test," our respondents must have been at least twenty-six years of age at the time of the first observation, and not over fifty-eight years (so that they will not be over seventy by the time of the terminal observation).

With these conditions stated, we can lend clearer meaning to the magnitudes of our actuarial "expected gain slopes" (the .0082 value in particular) by noting that we would need to be working with parent samples of well over 1,500 cases at each of the two endpoints in order to disentangle such effects reliably from calculable sampling error.[8] Since the SRC samples available as endpoints vary above and below the necessary case size, it is touch and go whether a naive investigator will arrive at the right answer or not, if a .05 level of significance is demanded.[9] The Gallup samples employed by Glenn do exceed this minimal case-number figure quite adequately, although as we have seen they do not measure the right variable and cannot be related to an underlying sampling theory in any strict way in any event.

In short, then, we can begin our own search for the age gains well apprised that even if these gains are large enough empirically to account for every last shred of the static age-strength relationship depicted in Figure 3, we shall have some little battle with sampling error on our hands before they can be laid bare in any satisfying way. And this means in turn that we can scarcely afford to follow the procedure of endpoint comparisons, which commits the ultimate sin of all data analysis by throwing away relevant information in quantities that are simply prodigal.

A Renewed Search for Age Gains. For my own cohort analysis of the strength component I shall work with the same fourteen national studies conducted by the Survey Research Center during the steady-state period that underlie Figure 3. These studies are somewhat irregularly spaced in time, but for all years save one (1959) there is at least one survey, and in one case (1964) there are three. In all, about 19,500 cases of party identification reports are available for this restricted period of observation.

Given this large mass of data, I have chosen to work with cohorts that are three years "wide." Let us restrict our attention to those cohorts that have a significant time series of identification strength values within the age limits from twenty-six to seventy.[10] Most of the younger cohorts enjoy 1,100-1,200 cases of independent observations, although this figure drops below 700 in the older groupings.

Since we have arrived at expectations stated in terms of slope per annum, what I propose to do is to estimate this slope as a function of time for each of our eligible cohorts. We shall most definitely not limit ourselves to a comparison of endpoints, however. After all, we have fourteen studies with which to work, and if we were to bring our case to rest by examining the differences between endpoint studies, we would be using information from only two of those studies. In other words, some 12/14ths of our information would be implicitly ignored, and as we have seen, we can scarcely afford this kind of waste.[11]

In principle, what we shall do instead is to estimate that slope for any given cohort simply by a least-squares solution for its average values, study by study, as a function of the passage of real time. In practice, I have entered one minor modification of such a procedure. Our fourteen samples are somewhat disparate in size, and hence in the stability of the estimates they are contributing to the time series for any given cohort. Indeed, in assembling the data it was apparent that the stray values in any given series tended to be associated with the smallest samples in the set, samples which yielded only a very limited number of cases for any given three-year cohort at any given point in real time. If I had extracted least-squares estimates for the already-grouped but otherwise raw data, no cognizance would be taken of this differential stability of estimates.[12] Therefore, for each cohort I have formed a time series of values which is itself a three-year moving average, weighted by the various N's contributing to that average. By such procedure, stray values from smaller studies make an appropriately smaller contribution to annual estimates than larger studies.

In this fashion I arrived at an estimate of a time slope in party strength for each of the thirteen cohorts fitting within our time interval. Let us consider what we expect of these per-annum slope values. We know in advance that even if a pure life-cycle effect has accounted for *all* of the observed static age-strength relationship, these slopes will only show faint positive values centering around the expectations of

.008 gain. Furthermore, with a constant eye on sampling error, we know that each of our individual cohort samples are based on a sufficiently-limited number of cases that the slope yielded by any given cohort will be subject to considerable error around such an expected value. In other words, while we would certainly expect the majority of our thirteen cohorts to show positive slopes, indicating a gain in identification strength with aging rather than a loss, it would be surprising if every cohort of the thirteen showed such a positive slope. Sampling error around the .008 expected value would lead us to expect a few stray cohorts to fall on the far side of zero, i.e., to have negative slopes. As always, to combat sampling error we must regain estimate strength by recombining case numbers, which means in this special case, inspecting the central tendency of the thirteen cohort-specific slope estimates.

Before we do this, we might note a few properties of our cohort-specific data which help relate them to the prior literature. If we look at our thirteen cohorts from the perspective of endpoint comparisons, we find that seven show a positive gain between the first and last study taken alone, while six show a negative difference, or loss in strength with aging, between the same endpoints. This is exactly the kind of finding that has provoked previous investigators to a final verdict that age gains cannot be demonstrated, and is a matter worth mention to assure the reader that our forth-coming conclusion—diametrically opposed—is not a mere product of some esoteric properties of the data file with which we are working, to which earlier investigators have not been privy.

If the summary score for endpoints is a lackluster 7-6, the case brightens considerably where slopes are concerned, registering a 10-3 verdict in favor of age gains. Moreover, two of the three negative slopes barely stray over the zero-point, and both occur late in the set of cohorts, when the underlying theory says that such gain slopes should be flattening down in any event. The reader should understand that the subjectively-large, if perhaps statistically paltry, change between the endpoint tally and the slope tally, comes as a result of taking all of the observations in our data file into account, rather than the 10-15 percent of them that happened to fall at the endpoints.

Nevertheless, all of these tallies remain a bit of bread and circuses. The truly important datum is the central tendency of these individual cohort slopes, a datum which throws all of our case numbers at the problem at once—almost 13,000 observations, rather than the mere thousand or so underlying each individual cohort slope estimate. *And this average slope turns out to be a positive .0076, which is a very good approximation of the .0082 which was to be expected if indeed life-cycle gains were the sole generating mechanism behind the static age-strength relationship.*[13] In short, for the appropriate period, the age gains in partisan strength are alive and well.

Table 1 presents the series of slope solutions for the set of individual cohorts. It makes the additional point that even the differential rate of gain by age—larger for the younger people, smaller for the older—finds support in this assembly of the data.

An Extended Denouement. Although this central result is simple enough, the problem remains complex and leaves us with a variety of loose ends to be surveyed. I feel painfully subject to one basic allegation. And this is that the whole empirical part of this demonstration is the purest tail-chasing: the numbers had to work out that way, and I knew it perfectly well before I started. After all, I dipped into the total corpus of the steady-state data to estimate, in an entirely actuarial way, what the expected age gains would have to be to account for the observed static relationship. Then, incestuously enough, I returned to the same body of data, sliced them slightly differently (by aging cohort), and came up with an entirely parallel result. Since I was working

TABLE 1: Changes in Strength of Party Identification with Aging
Over the 1952-1964 Period, by Birth Cohort

	Cohort (By Birth Date)	Gain Per Annum in Mean Party Identi- fication Strength (Slope)
"PURE"	1929–1931	.0350
EARLY	1926–1928	.0179
SEGMENT	1923–1925	−.0185
	1920–1922	.0003
(Data between	1917–1919	.0223
ages of 26	1914–1916	.0060
and 52)	1911–1913	.0014
Subtotals	Observed Mean Slope:	.0092
	Expected Mean Slope:	.0108
	1908–1910	.0055
LATER	1905–1907	.0180
(OLDER)	1902–1904	.0135
SEGMENT	1899–1901	−.0029
	1896–1898	.0025
	1893–1895	−.0025
Subtotals	Observed Mean Slope:	.0057
	Expected Mean Slope:	.0056
GRAND TOTALS:	OBSERVED MEAN SLOPE, 13 COHORTS	.0076
	EXPECTED MEAN SLOPE	.0082

within the terms of a logical necessity to begin with, the results are scarcely exciting: they are humdrum and close to tautological.

I am especially sensitive to such a criticism, because I myself have felt alternately sheepish and annoyed at being obliged to push these numbers around at such length, for exactly the reasons cited. My defenses are three, which I shall lay out in ascending order of importance.

The first defense simply involves the state of understanding of these matters in the discipline. The Crittenden decade was painful in its complete misconstruction of the cohort verdict for the direction component of party identification. With the discipline now threatening to converge on what is essentially a logical impossibility as the proper revisionist verdict for the strength component, it seemed necessary to say something.

The second defense involves a deeper bite into the substantive problem. The chain of reasoning which has led prior analysts to adopt the generational view of the age-strength relationship is always the same, and thoroughly perplexing. For each, the most lively hypothesis is that of age gains. Hence the data are intensively examined in order to locate those gains; and tests, in at least a loose sense of the word, are performed toward their confirmation. The results are construed as null. Hence the reputed age gains do not exist. Ergo, and without any corresponding test, the static age-strength relationship is pronounced to be a generational matter, involving differences in early socialization which will ever leave their imprint on the cohorts involved.[14]

It is obvious that this rival hypothesis can be subjected to quite the same test as the age-gain hypothesis. And it is my distinct impression that while the age-gain evidence is admittedly undistinguished to any casual glance, the parallel evidence for the generational verdict is a total loss. Indeed, I believe that had prior analysts bothered to test that hypothesis before proclaiming its truth, they would rapidly have come to understand the proper dimensions of the problem.

To complete the logical circle, therefore, I have in fact duplicated the preceding analysis, but now run the other way, as a less circumstantial evaluation of the Glenn-Abramson verdict. In other words, still operating under the simple-effects assumption, I have examined the evidence for the proposition that during the steady-state period, the shape of the static age-strength relationship was determined by the fact that people socialized into political partisanship in an earlier (turn-of-the-century) America were imprinted with stronger identifications than has been true in more recent eras of child-rearing.

Always assuming no more than simple effects, an appropriate test involves organizing the data in a form whereby birth year varies but chronological age is kept constant. For such an assembly, I have again computed slopes by birth year for these cohorts, and averaged them as before. If the generational construction has merit, then we should find that the average slope is positive, assuming that by "positive" we mean that the earlier the birth year, the stronger the partisan identification. In fact, if the Glenn-Abramson conclusion could equally well account for the static age-strength relationship observed in the steady-state period, these slopes should again center on a value of .008 per annum.

Without boring the reader with details, the actual average slope, keyed in the direction stated, turns out to be −.001. It is absurd to construe this number as other than the flattest of zeroes; but if we were obliged to pay attention to the negative sign, even the direction is contrary to what Glenn and Abramson concluded from their looser inspection of the data.

Such a result is not at all astonishing. If by tracing the aging of cohorts over time we have found almost exactly the magnitude of age gains necessary to understand the total slope involved in the static relationship, it would have been troublesome indeed to have found that a generational construction could account equally well, or even partially, for the contours of that relationship. It is far more pleasing to find that with the liberty of a little rounding, *generation essentially accounts for none at all.*

This result squares more nicely than might appear at first glance with the parallel Knoke and Hout (1974) findings. These investigators are using the proportion identifying, rather than our expression of mean strength, as the key dependent variable. Moreover, their data are considerably more refined for this test of generation effects, since they estimate them with period, life-cycle and seven other sociostructural variables controlled. However, none of these differences in procedure appear to be responsible for any major differences in conclusions, since my data show the same contours as do theirs. The fact that they find significant generation effects, in addition to a principal life-cycle effect, is the result of quite another difference in their treatment.

The Knoke-Hout residual variance associated uniquely with generation (1974: 707, col. 6, "Cohort") looks much the cross-section of a soup bowl, with an extended center of fifteen cohorts with minimal variation, and a "lip" at either end, consisting of three cohorts with much higher rates of independence. Of these two lips, it is the one at the young end which is contributing to most of the "explained variance." This is true because the deviations to the young side are absolutely sharper than the lip at the "old" end of the spectrum, and more especially because the three cohorts forming the young lip are populated with nearly 1,300 cases, whereas there is only a sparse total of less than 180 cases sprinkled over the three cohorts forming the less dramatic lip at the other (old) end. Therefore when we recognize that the Knoke-Hout data embrace the full 1952-1972 period, whereas my calculations are by design restricted to the steady-state period through 1964 only, it is easy to see that the influential lip to the young side of the Knoke-Hout spectrum is essentially clipped away by such a restriction. This leaves mainly the flat bottom of the soup bowl, with its minor and uninterpretable variation, along with the sparsely populated lip at the old end of the spectrum.

I have nearly the same slight rise in independence (or decline in strength) for cohorts of pre-1880 birth, despite the fact that I have somewhat more cases and a different version of the dependent variable. Indeed, it is this slight reversal that sets my average slope calculation faintly negative (−.001), since it runs counter to the expectation that older cohorts were more strongly socialized into partisanship. It is a moot point whether this anomaly is substantial enough to be of theoretical interest.[15] But the important point for the moment is that anomaly or no, these data flatly refute the Glenn-Abramson conclusions as to the source of the age-strength relationship in the steady-state period.

Although all of these results fit delectably with what we took to be the pure logic of the matter for the steady-state period in our discussion in Chapter 2, such logic rests on assumptions. And while I took some pains to lay these out at the beginning, it is now high time to review them. Three of the four ingredients of that logic remain unimpeachable, resting as they do on empirical features of the situation which nobody contests. But the status of the fourth assumption is less self-evident. This is the assumption that whatever shaped the static age-strength relationship of this period, the generating effects were simple ones where possible cohort verdicts are concerned.

A review of this assumption in particular constitutes my third defense of what might otherwise appear to be a tail-chasing operation. I have demonstrated that within the terms of a simple-effects assumption, there is no serious question as to what competing effects the data insist on setting to zero and what remaining effect is responsible for all of the static age relationship. That much is in hand. Furthermore, since any assumption of simple effects is subject to controversy, I feel that we have done more. *The clarity of the empirical demonstration itself,* which strictly speaking is not entirely tail-chasing given the softness of one assumption involved, acts back to lend some provisional credence to that assumption, be it ever so soft.

Here we must be careful. I am not saying that the clarity of the empirical demonstration has *proved,* in the normal sense of the word, that only one simple effect is involved. I am saying much more modestly that the observed data are handsomely compatible with the possibility that only one simple effect—life-cycle age gains—was shaping the static age-strength relationship during this period. In other words, it is not quite true that our numbers had to work out the way they did: if any of a range of complex effects were governing these processes, they could have worked out differently.

Nonetheless, nothing we have done outflanks the fundamental indeterminacy involved, since other complex combinations of life-cycle and generational effects could still be compatible with the same total configuration of cohort data. We are undoubtedly well ahead of the game, for some other lively possibilities—such as the simple-effect, generational possibility—seem conclusively disproved as incompatible with the observed data. But proof of the certainty of simple-effect age gains, we have not.

With all this duly said, let us now descend to the level of common sense. There is no question that an important edge of indeterminacy remains, or that we have failed to provide normally compelling proof of simple age-gain effects as the prime generator of partisan strength in this period. But as soon as we begin to introduce, in the face of a fundamental indeterminacy, considerations of plausibility, not to mention parsimony, then it would seem that a simple-effect interpretation of the steady-state period has entirely the upper hand.

It is clear that one could construct a process model involving delicate interactions between generational, period and life-cycle effects which might serve to simulate all the known features of the steady-state period, where identification strength is concerned. It would be an interesting parlor exercise to see what such a model would look like. Among other things, it would have to have certain outcomes in equilibrium, in order to reproduce the several aggregate constancies of the steady-state period. I would not challenge its plausibility on those grounds, since many complex social forces seem, more often than not, to strike an aggregate equilibrium, and indeed one such equilibrium, although the fairly obvious one of pure "demographic metabolism," has to be involved even with the simple-effects, life-cycle model. Nonetheless, I suspect that such a model, while constructible, would entail a whole congeries of postulated effects that were far more numerically dictated than theoretically motivated; and that such a complex model as a totality would find little resonance in any of the side information which a familiarity with the subject matter can bring to bear on the problem.

Meanwhile, the simple-effects solution does have some substantive articulation with other things that are known. There is, for example, now massive evidence that a variety of evaluations and perceptions that Americans had maintained of their government and life in the society in fairly constant form in the post-war period suddenly began to unravel in the middle of the 1960s, contemporaneous with the apparent onset of uncommon period effects bearing on the strength of partisan identification.[16]

I shall not dwell here upon these interlocking changes of the 1960s, for they will be part of our focus in the next chapter. For the moment, I propose to accept a simple-effect hypothesis of life-cycle gains as fully accounting for the static relationship between age and strength of party identification during the steady-state period, 1952-1964, at least until a construction as compelling, if necessarily more complex, is proposed. I am anxious to take such a tool in a serious way, even as a working hypothesis, in order to see of what help it may be in improving our understanding as to the cohort dynamics of the strength component after the termination of the steady-state period in 1964.

NOTES

1. Actually, there may be a significant increase in the *variance* of the strength measure among the very old in the United States, which underlies the flattening mean. That is, some among the very old seem to get increasingly dogmatic about the pure strength of their identification while at the same time

the proportions registering as "zero" on the scale—independent or apolitical—grows as well, apparently reflecting the increased psychological disengagement of some elderly from politics. In other words, in these oldest cohorts the proportion who describe themselves with intermediate strengths continues to decline, although the gains in "strong" identifiers are being offset by the gains in the proportions taking themselves out of consideration with "independent" and "apolitical" responses.

2. The function in Figure 3 naturally becomes increasingly irregular after age sixty or so because case numbers are thinning out rapidly and sampling error is increasing correspondingly. The irregularities prior to age twenty-six cannot, however, be understood in these terms.

3. The core of the problem centers among males, and particularly black males in these age ranges.

4. These estimates are based, needless to say, upon comparisons with Census tables whose own underenumerations have themselves already been corrected.

5. One discordant fact is that while the hook is persistent enough during the steady-state period, it seems to have been withering away in very recent years. This is definitely not because of any marked improvement in sampling this first cohort. It would seem that either the dramatic steepening of the strength function in the earliest cohort since 1964 is obscuring the effect; or that amid other changes in identification patterns in the recent period, the underlying relationship between transience and identification may have weakened. While the interpretation of the phenomenon is far from a closed book at this point, the lack of reliability of data from the first cohorts remains uncontestable.

6. A reasonable fit for the observed curve in Figure 3 is an expression like

$$y = 2.27 - 1.12 \, e^{-.3x},$$

where y is the mean strength of party identification in the scalar currency being used, and x is the chronological age of the cohort in years.

7. Here and at a couple of later points, it should be clear that less approximate methods might be used. However, working under some technological limitations at the time these basic analyses were done, we settled for these analytic choices. Even these approximations are far more incisive than methods employed in earlier cohort analyses, and as we shall see are quite adequate for the task without prejudicing the case one way or another.

8. The major "cost" factors being recognized in this estimate include standard sampling error of a simple random sample sort, as expanded by a reasonable "design effect" multiplier (Kish, 1965) to take account of the fact that all of these sampling designs are geographically clustered; and the case attrition which necessarily arises because nearly 30 percent of any such parent sample will be ineligible for inclusion in the test.

9. Quite naturally, the proper "trends" should be present in such data. The touch-and-go nature of the result is well reflected in the fact that several scholars have told us informally that they have confirmed the existence of age gains with SRC data, although they did not bother to write it up because it was not "news." Wrong results have a disturbing "survival value" in the march to publication, simply because of their novelty.

10. It should be noted that in an effort to preserve as many cases as possible for our critical estimates, we have included (as an extreme of a three-year cohort) a birth-year cohort which was not twenty-six until as late as 1957. Values reported from these youngest cohorts are ignored until they are in fact twenty-six years of age. All this means is that one youngest cohort provides only an abbreviated time series of eight years (midpoint) rather than twelve. A similar slight truncation was used for persons passing age seventy near the end of the observation period.

11. I do not intend to imply that prior analysts have labored to assemble large files of cohort data, and then set all but the first and last studies aside. In all instances, the analysts have indeed laid out the relevant time series of identification strengths, cohort by cohort, and subjected them to at least private visual inspection, usually displaying them publicly. But the analyst who has been trained to expect to see age gains, anticipates that the strength values will march briskly up the page as the cohort age increases. Instead he finds a graph that looks like nothing so much as a cross-section profile of swamp grass. It is inevitable that he is looking at almost pure sampling error.

It should be made clear why this happens. We have already seen that the age-gain "signals" over a twelve-year period are barely discernible by end-point comparisons even with total N's for test cases (a fraction of the parent sample) which number well over 1,000. By visually inspecting the full time series, rather than looking only at endpoints, the investigator is vastly strengthening his case numbers. However, he has at the same time (in inspecting individual cohorts) sliced his overall N by an average factor of six, or eight, or ten, depending on the number of cohorts chronicled. Thus working at the cohort level his sampling error has itself increased by some factor between, say, 2½ and 4, and he is at least back where he started, and more likely worse off, save as he develops some means of recombining his information over cohorts once again.

Boggled by the lack of any detectible visual pattern, he either publishes the series and invites the reader to note how little pattern there is, or he resorts to endpoint summaries of cohort gains and loses, to quantify the absence of age gains. The latter strategy is frequent enough that we feel entitled to comment upon it: it has the merit of regaining some case strength by summarizing across cohorts; but it immediately tosses that advantage into the wind by ignoring the vast majority of the time series observations available.

12. It should be clear that this modification was occasioned purely because we were working with grouped values (the mean for cohort i at time t) and a desk calculator. With individual-level data and a computer, this modification would be unnecessary.

13. It might also be noted that were we to delete the thirteenth cohort, which was approaching seventy in this period, the remaining mean would be .0084!

14. To date I have found only one kind of casual reference which purports to provide an empirical base for accepting the generational hypothesis (as opposed to rejecting a version of the life-cycle one). This is the observation that where identification strength is concerned "intercohort differences are much larger than intracohort ones" (my paraphrase). Such a datum is construed as supporting a generational interpretation. If the reader has been following my argument up to

this point, he should see plainly that such an observation has almost nothing to do with the issue at all. I grant that in my data, as in all others I have seen, intercohort differences in strength considerably outweigh intracohort ones. I would also observe that under conditions prevailing (twelve years to track intracohort differences, in the better "tests," and a sixty-year field of vision across cohorts), the intercohort differences *should* be about five times as great as the intracohort differences *even if there is no generational variation whatever, and the total static relationship is a product of pure life-cycle accumulations.*

15. Actually, in preparing the original draft of this part of this paper a year or more before the appearance of the Knoke-Hout article, I had puzzled for a long time over whether to mention this anomaly or to write it off as sampling error. I had finally decided to ignore it, for the combined Bayesian reason that the case numbers are very thin, and a wide variety of evidence of other kinds suggests that political socialization prior to 1890 or 1900 was much more religiously partisan than any in the twentieth century. Knoke and Hout do develop this anomaly into a substantive point, however, and I am sympathetic to such a temptation. Perhaps the most stunning lesson, and surely the most robust one, that arises from the generational side of these analyses is the lack of support for any contention, frequently made, that partisan socialization has declined in its vigor secularly over the whole course of the twentieth century prior to the major decline after 1965. There is absolutely no sign of such an effect, and indeed the data carry back with at least fair reliability to persons of age ten as early as 1880 or 1885.

16. For an excellent summary of these changes which is both panoramic and usefully analytical, see Nie, Verba and Petrocik (1976).

Chapter 4

THE STRENGTH COMPONENT AFTER 1964

Up to this point, our discussion has tried to keep eyes in two directions at once. I have been interested in addressing a very central substantive issue concerning the cross-time dynamics displayed by variations in intensity of loyalties to one or the other of the major political parties. I have also paid a great deal of explicit attention, along the way, to a whole series of more purely methodological problems that surround the strategy and tactics of cohort inference.

As we turn from the steady-state period to the era of political crisis which has beset the country in the past decade, it would be natural to become less methodological and more historically descriptive. It has been, after all, an "intensely historical" period. I shall resist that temptation, however, and if anything will lean still further in a methodological direction. Obviously, I shall not eschew descriptive detail in the process, and indeed must dwell upon some gross features of the period which, if not already familiar to the reader, may well have lively substantive interest. Nonetheless, I will be content to leave the center of gravity on the methodological side.

I shall do so for two simple reasons. One is that a variety of descriptive works treating the decline of partisanship after 1964 are already in the literature. Indeed, Glenn (1972) and Abramson (1976) devote major attention to the descriptive features of this period, and I am happy to recommend their treatments of it. While I shall indeed find a stray point or two of fact or interpretation at which my own results diverge, these are never of any central consequence. Most of the primary substantive findings merely duplicate their work, and so I shall avoid the descriptive embroidery to minimize redundancy.

On the other hand, I see a more methodologically-oriented treatment of the period as a positive opportunity, because of the cards which the tricks of history have placed in our hands at this point. In the first chapter of this book, I pointed out the fundamental indeterminacy of cohort analysis, and opined that the only reasonable salvation for the analyst lay in side information about the subject matter at hand. I tried to convey the notion that while any compelling side information, of any provenience, should be regarded as precious in this game, certain kinds of side information do not lie so very far "outside" the batch of cohort data itself.

We encountered some tangible glimmers of this possibility in Chapter 2, where we were able to arrive at some provisional cohort diagnoses without even doing a cohort analysis in the normal sense of the word. However, that was a fortuitous result in a very special case, and nothing of much generality. We are now arrived, however, at a more pregnant point of the same general type.

If we accept the plausibility conclusions of the preceding chapter concerning the dynamics of the steady-state period, then we are bound to conclude that whatever else is true, the period after 1964 is certain to be more complex, and hence more treacherously indeterminate for any effort at cohort inference. Given the amount of stumbling that has characterized scholarly efforts at the relevant cohort diagnoses for the direction and strength components of party identification within the simplicity of the steady-state period, this does not bode well for analyses of the more recent period.

However, since the confines of the situation itself force us to trade heavily in plausibilities and side information to make any progress at all, we might thank history for providing us in this special case with at least one simple period, before the deluge. In other words, it is worth exploring the possibility that highly plausible results from one particularly felicitous segment of a cohort time series can be used as side information to restrict some of the heightened ambiguities that cloud a less felicitous segment of the same cohort time series, dealing as always in terms of plausibilities, rather than proof positive. In short, they may help to give us "a place to stand."

This chapter comes in three parts. In the first part we shall simply take stock of the gross features of the post-1964 period which seem most relevant for cohort analysis, much as we did in Chapter 2 for the steady-state period. The second part will draw us deeper into the details of cohorts in this period, with a focus on what moderately-generalizable information we might extract from this crisis period, to help cohort analyses of similar subject matters. The final portion of the chapter will be spent in foolhardy extrapolation, based on what we have learned.

The Onset of Period Effects

We have seen from Figure 1 that at some time between late in 1964 and late in 1966, the steady-state period of aggregate constancy in party identification strength was disturbed by a major downturn in identification strength which has proceeded almost majestically to the current writing (1975).

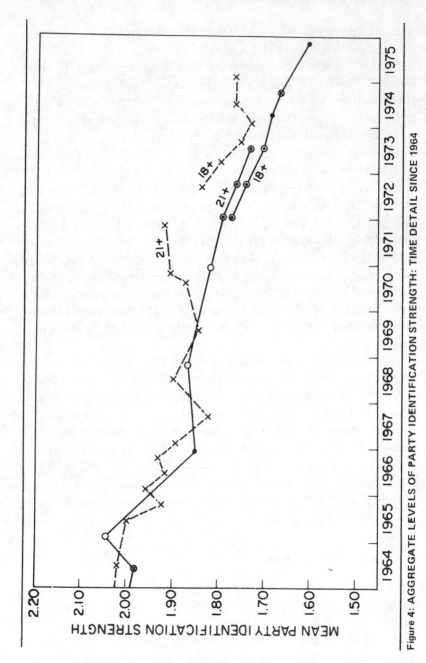

Figure 4: AGGREGATE LEVELS OF PARTY IDENTIFICATION STRENGTH: TIME DETAIL SINCE 1964

To illuminate this period we have at our disposal cohort files of data from twelve national samples conducted after early 1965 by the Survey Research Center, usually although not always for the Center for Political Studies. This portion of the file contains nearly 19,000 cases. Although these studies are reasonably sprinkled over the full decade from 1966 to 1975, with never more than a two-year gap between readings, the great weight of case numbers—about three-quarters—lies in the second half of this period. If we had to encounter such a maldistribution, it is probably just as well that the richest numbers lie near the end of the period, since the series is bounded on its front side by the massive bases for estimation provided by the steady-state period. Thus the endpoints are well-anchored. However, the thinness of the early part of the record will prove troublesome for our analyses at several critical points. The 1966 study, which involved less than 1,300 cases and is the smallest in the series, is a particularly weak link, and one without backing for nearly two years on either side.

Timing of the Downturn. Figure 1 suggests that the turning-point ending the steady-state period was quite abrupt, and it is of great interest to date this turning-point as precisely as possible, within the accepted 1964-1966 range. In Figure 4 we have stretched out the time axis of Figure 1, in order to have a closer look at this matter.[1]

The SRC 1964 Election Study had shown normal steady-state values for party identification. In January and February of 1965, the Economic Behavior Program of the Center had a relatively large (N over 2,100) study in the field which included the standard item. Although the aggregate mean lay within reasonable sampling error of the steady-state mean, the absolute values were actually *higher* than usual, and among the highest in the whole series dating back to 1952.[2] Thus there was no sign of the imminent turning-point as late as February, 1965, and the next SRC sample using the item was not until December, 1966, when the new trend was already well underway.

Although the Gallup political affiliation question is not the same item, it tracks well enough with the SRC item over time, particularly in the critical period, that the more densely distributed Gallup measurements provide highly useful further information. Gallup results dated June, 1965, while showing levels slightly lower than the next preceding studies, remain well within the band of observations defining the steady state. But by the next published results, dated October 1965, the trend had moved sharply downward, never to return to the steady-state level (Figure 4). Thus the summer of 1965 seems reasonably well documented as the actual turning-point.

Period Effects vs. Competing Explanations. It is hard to see a downturn this abrupt and unusual without concluding that a response to the immediate events of the historical period is involved rather than, say, the more gradual and stately movements associated with demographic shifts. Moreover, there seems to be no particular controversy about such a verdict. Nonetheless, it is worth spending a few introductory moments to clear away some small underbrush of competing possibilities, and to establish the sense in which the the post-1964 behavior of the strength component appears to have been responsive to what are in the strictest sense "period effects," following the definitions of our first chapter.

During the 1950s and early 1960s, it was easy to foresee that the aggregate strength of identifications in the electorate would decline in some degree in the later 1960s. This is so simply because the baby boom of the period at the end of World War II could be counted on to break upon the adult electorate after the middle 1960s, significantly lowering the average age of the eligible citizenry. If the parameters of the steady-state period were to hold, such a lowering would automatically entail a decline in aggregate strength. Furthermore, by the later 1960s the enfranchising of eighteen-year-olds on a full national scale (as opposed to a scattering of less populous states like Georgia and Kentucky) was coming into view, a change which could be counted on to push the strength component lower still.

These are pure compositional effects. There is nothing unreal about them, of course, but neither is there any point in getting their effects confused with those dynamics of cohort development that are our major problem of inference here.[3] Figure 1, being defined specifically in terms of the eligible electorate at each point in time (including eighteen-year-olds nationally starting in 1972) is not constructed to aid in this kind of discrimination. And at least casual suggestions have been made to the effect that the declines registered in Figure 1 might be entirely understood in terms of such pure compositional change.

It is intriguing, of course, that the 1965 downturn in strength levels coincides almost exactly with the entry of the first baby-boom cohorts into the eligible electorate. However, I know of no scholars who have examined the matter at all closely who would maintain that such pure compositional effects can account for the observed change. All would agree, presumably, that both the changing age table and the reduced voting age make some contribution to the overall decline. But even in combination they do not begin to explain the fading identification strength of the electorate.

Fortunately, the evidence on this score is extremely easy to develop and is not vulnerable to the kinds of indeterminacies that shadow other kinds of cohort inference. It is easy enough to remove the eighteen through twenty year-old voters from the later data, to ask how the electorate would look without their intrusion. Similarly, it is possible to normalize the later data against the contours of pre-baby-boom age tables to estimate the relevant effects on aggregate levels of identification.

In fact, I have carried out such an operation out of curiosity, recalculating the aggregate strength shown by twenty-one-and-over adults as of 1972 on the basis of the age table from the 1960 Census. While the difference in the two estimates (both excluding those eighteen through twenty) runs in the right direction, as it must, the magnitude of the difference is infinitesimal, being little more than enough visually to discriminate two separate points on a graph of the scale of Figure 1. Clearly the compositional change flowing from the baby boom has had almost nothing to do with the decline of the strength component.[4]

The lowering of the voting age made a somewhat stronger contribution to the overall decline. However, as one can see from the brief "splicing" we have added to Figure 4, even these effects added to the baby boom at most account for a very limited fraction of the observed net aggregate change: up through 1972, probably one part in six would be a generous estimate of the contribution. In sum, the bulk of the net change simply cannot be traced to these kinds of compositional shifts and redefinitions.

If most of the observed effect is historical in the broad sense of population responses to current events, then it still remains for us to specify more precisely which type of historical impact is at stake. In the first chapter we were able to discriminate two types of change fitting under this historical rubric. These two types, the classic generational as opposed to "period effects," can readily be distinguished as ideal types, although I have already suggested that there may be a considerable area of blur between them. Fortunately, for once the gray is more conceptual than operational, so that we can continue to develop certain kinds of unequivocal statements.

The classic generational effect, as I am using the term, involves by definition a kind of early imprinting which, while it may be overlaid by other kinds of effects, including life-cycle ones, during the life span, will always leave its characteristic mark as a deviation of the generation affected from neighboring generational cohorts. The prototype here is the set of purely genetic effects, although for cultural attitudes like party identification (including the strength component), the analogue lies with early political socialization. "Period effects," on the other hand, arise when historical events provoke relevant changes among "children of all ages," including the eighty-year olds.

The first question we can ask of these historic intrusions, then, is whether they are leaving their marks in changed attitudes toward the parties among citizens who were already adults and in the electorate before the intrusions began to be felt; or whether they can be traced exclusively to far weaker identifications among incoming cohorts than was true in the past, such that as these replacements loom larger and larger in the total adult electorate, the aggregate strength of identification dwindles. That incoming cohorts have indeed dropped off remarkably in their partisanship is known to be true; but the crucial question remains whether this influx is sufficient to account for the total decline in Figure 1, or at least that part of it not already intelligible in terms of compositional effects.

If one happened to have a proper grasp of the magnitude of the variances involved, one could reject with a glance at Figure 1 that the total change which has registered could be tracked to incoming cohorts alone, even if all new voters were entering the system as pure independents (which, of course, they were not). This is true simply because those fresh additions, particularly in the early part of the period, were woefully inadequate numerically to make any major dent in a mean based on the total electorate. Even though the two annual cohorts that were eligible to vote for their first national election in 1966 were large, relative to prior entering cohorts, they were only a tiny fraction of the total base, and hence could only add the faintest coloration to total-electorate data.

There is no reason to leave the matter at such a deduction, however, and Figure 5 makes the case entirely plain. To the earlier function for the total electorate, we have simply

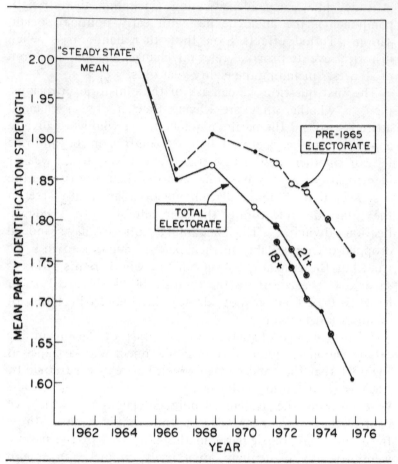

Figure 5: AGGREGATE LEVELS OF PARTY IDENTIFICATION STRENGTH
SINCE 1964, BY SEGMENTS OF THE ELECTORATE

added the relevant curve based exclusively on cohorts that
were already eligible electors prior to 1965 (born in 1943 or
before). This curve automatically removes all effects due to
cohorts entering the system after 1964, as well as all
compositional effects (the change the baby boom bestowed
on the adult life table, along with the eighteen-year-old
enfranchisement) associated with those cohorts. The latter-

day behavior of the two curves are naturally of interest in Figure 5, we shall return to this somewhat later. For now we merely wish to focus on the early portion of the period, and here the figure attests quite eloquently that while the growing influx of weakly-identifying young cohorts is pro-gressively amplifying the original change, virtually all of that change initially registered as a pure period effect in the strict sense of our definition, i.e., among persons already in the electorate and displaying normal parameters of the steady-state period prior to the new historical intrusion. This much seems unequivocal.

Although we can very close to guarantee (with any simple-model assumptions, at any rate) that period effects were one type of major historical input, does this in any sense rule out the more classic form of the generational hypothesis, involving new entrants with initial values de-parting from those of earlier entrants, as making a contri-bution to the situation?

Clearly it does not, although this is the point at which we begin to move into the conceptual grays. We can rule out such generational effects as being the prime mover in the change, from the simplest inspection of Figure 5. Yet it is also true that the new entrants do have different initial values, and hence that some generation-like effects are making about as much contribution as they could to the situation.

The grays begin to cloud the situation when we find we must ask, in order to make any strict division between adult response to a historic situation and the imprint of earlier socialization borne by entering cohorts, "how early is early?" Do we class as generational effects absolutely all influences that shape the near-novitiate, right down to the very eve of his entry into the system; or by "early socialization" do we really mean instead postures that were laid down, in the kind of case we have at hand, considerably before the age of seventeen or twenty? More to the point, perhaps, how can we even tell at what presystem point the distinctive attitudes were formed, since we usually only see them for the first time upon actual entry?

Let us start the argument at the far end, dealing first with classic generational effects in their most nearly pure form, involving an initial and early accumulation of ideas about, and attitudes toward, what are in this case national political parties.[5] There is ample empirical reason to imagine that such truly "early" socialization is well underway by the time the child is seven or eight, and is in a form which is recognizable relative to adult data by the ages of thirteen or fourteen. This does not mean that all relevant learning has ceased by the latter ages, and the relevant identifications are demonstrably more labile than they become later. Nonetheless, if we are referring to "early socialization" specifically because such learning is alleged to have peculiarly strong imprinting powers, then these are surely the ages we must have in mind.

Now let us return to the data with such a definition in mind. To explain the fact that cohorts entering the electorate in 1965 or 1966 and thereafter were unusually low in partisanship in terms of a distinctive early socialization, we would be obliged to imagine that the standard agents of socialization—mainly the family, but also the schools, peers, etc.—must have begun altering the image they were conveying of the citizen's relationship to his political party no later than 1958 or so. Of course there is absolutely no reason to imagine that such a change took place historically, although none of our data can rule it out. What would be most striking in such a scenario, however, would be the enormous coincidence that just at the exact moment when these distinctively-socialized cohorts began to enter the electorate in 1965 or 1966 for the first time, a large number of older cohorts, demonstrably not so socialized, suddenly had a change of heart about the political parties so that their declining strengths of attachment were exactly continuous, in adjacent age groupings,[6] with the distinctive new attitudes of that entering cohort!

As usual, we cannot definitively disprove such a scenario; but the reader will not be surprised to learn that I find it toweringly implausible. In other words, I am prepared to reject the distinctiveness of incoming cohorts after 1964 as any proof that the pure "early-socialization" version of the generational hypothesis was *also* a contributing influence to the downturn in identification strengths marking the late 1960s. It seems far preferable to imagine that young people who were nineteen and twenty in 1964 entered the 1966 electorate with weaker identifications not because of some distinctive earlier socialization, but rather because they were responding in exactly the same ways (although a bit more so) to the same national events that touched off the 1965 decline among other young people in their twenties who had voted in 1964. And if we call the latter a "period effect," as opposed to a "generational effect," then it would seem at least artificial, if not haplessly confusing, to insist that the former effect was instead "generational" on the technicality that the persons so affected were still some months short of entering the system.

None of this is to argue, of course, that "period effects" are nongenerational, or ahistorical, in the broader meanings of those terms. Obviously, they have their peculiar effects on those generations of all ages who, as an historical matter, happen to be exposed to them. Nor is it to argue that the perturbations of the 1960s which, in a cohort-analytic context, we shall insist on identifying as period effects, will for ever and ever be insulated from anything one might want to identify as a "generational" effect in a strict, early-socialization sense. In fact, quite to the contrary. If a distinct generation in the late 1960s suffered a peculiar onset of disenchantment about their party commitments due to any number of national events, it would scarcely be surprising if such less enthusiastic attitudes were conveyed to the much younger cohort (e.g., those born in the 1951-1960 period) whose early socialization the young adults of the 1960s are conducting. Thus in due time the period effects of the latter 1960s may well have an impact toward actual changes in early socialization. However, there are delays involved by definition in the fruition of such developments; and although they may be impending almost as we write, they can logically have had almost nothing to do with any of the changes registered in the period covered by this text.

The reader who has managed to bear with us over the past half-dozen paragraphs is likely to be on the brink of asking wryly who is responsible for insisting on the conceptual partition between "period effects" and "generational effects," since it seems to verge on a distinction without a difference. Certainly such a discrimination is far hazier than that between either type of generational phenomenon and true life-cycle effects. Yet we must remember at the same time that in current understandings of the cohort inference problem, the distinction is absolutely crucial. It is what turns a problem involving two classes of effects into one of three effects. Given the presence of only two diagnostic variables, the distinction transforms a tractable problem into an intractable one, and that is no minor boundary.

It is because of the continuities between "period effects" and "generational effects" that there is a sense in which less than three independent classes of effects are involved. This fact does not solve the problem, as we shall see later that there are other senses in which more than three distinctive variables may be involved. However this may be, if we must deal in plausibilities in any event, then to come to the problem armed with the likelihood that period effects tend to register continuously across adjacent cohorts, even very young ones; or that today's period effects may often impact on socialization practices to become tomorrow's generation effects; then all of these observations provide welcome side information toward more compelling diagnoses.

A Cohort Analysis of Period Effects

Once again, as in Chapter 2, we have arrived at a fairly clear cohort-effect diagnosis without as yet descending into the particulars of a full cohort analysis. That is to say, with no more than the crude kind of cohort dichotomy represented in Figure 5 we have established to within reasonable satisfaction that where the post-1964 era is concerned we are dealing with period effects, much more than with classic generational effects, although the two tend to merge in a disconcerting way at their mutual boundaries.

What we might profitably do next is a kind of second-order cohort analysis. That is, with a period-effect verdict already in hand as by far the most plausible, it is worthwhile to go on to analyze the relative impact of this period, again by detailed cohort.

There is important purpose here, even for the more general problem of cohort inference. Despite the fact that the history of party identification after 1964 in the United States is no more than a special case of the problem, it is through the accumulation of many such special cases that we have a chance to amass side information concerning what is more and less plausible in these matters. The kind of side information that now interests us is of the following sort. When period effects strike a population, are they more likely to impact upon it in some way rather than others? More particularly, it would be useful to know whether there are characteristic forms of such impact across the life span, since this information is most relevant for the cohort problem. Formally speaking, then, we can ask whether there are any likely interaction effects between the impact of a given period on some attribute and the age of the actor at the time he experiences the period in question.

If period effects are touched off by "events," in at least a broad sense of the word, then it goes without saying that their impact on any given actor depends in the first instance on the knowledge that they have occurred. Since exposure to such information is never absolutely guaranteed, and indeed in some cases may be quite problematic, this observation is a fundamental one. Japanese soldiers emerging from Pacific jungles a decade or two after the end of World War II without knowledge that the war had ended, could not have been expected to have experienced characteristic redefinitions of the situation in the late 1940s. However important the observation, I shall pass by it in some haste, on grounds that in the case of party identification we are dealing with broad-scale societal events and drifts to which exposure of the population has been nearly total. This does not mean it has been complete to the last sentient member of the population; but in the degree that margins of nonexposure exist, it will suffice for our purposes if sheer exposure can be taken as essentially constant by actor age. And, aside from problems of senility, that seems a reasonable assumption in this special case.

It is useful to think of the problem in terms of a simple graph in which population members are arrayed on the abscissa by their chronological age at the time the impacting events occurred, with the relative severity of the impact, in terms of degree of attribute change, represented on the ordinate.

If we approach the problem tabula rasa, there is of course no limit on the possible forms such an impact function might take. One form would be a simple rectangle, saying that response to the period impact was of equal direction and magnitude for population members of all ages experiencing it. In other words, impact and age would be unrelated, and there would be no special interactions to be accounted for between age and period effects. There is nothing intrinsically implausible about such a function. Another form might be the infinite set of chaotic ones, in which responses to the impact bounce up and down in utterly bewildering fashion from one annual cohort (or, for that matter, monthly cohort) to the next, without even a trace of periodicity in highs and lows over the life span. Such a set of forms is surely possible, but would not rank very high in plausibility.

As usual, there are distinct advantages in not approaching the problem tabula rasa, but rather with some sensible attention to the substance of the matter at hand. Many types of societal "events" (still broadly construed) have intrinsic and obvious age-specific consequences. The launching of a military draft is one. The bankruptcy of an old-age social security system is another. We would be foolish to imagine that all "period effects" flowing from such events, whatever the dependent variable in question, would show impact functions perfectly compartmentalized by limited chronological age. Anticipations are stirred on the front side of the statutory ages involved, and memories on the back side. People are also linked together in social relationships, and the parents of draft-age children are especially vulnerable to the onset of concerns, as are the children of bankrupted pensioners. But the important point is that if main effects and spill-over effects stand as contours on our age-impact function, all of these kinds of side information create some very plausible expectations about the shape of that function in the special case, and in so doing challenge the plausibility of an infinite number of others.

When we turn to the special case of party identification in these terms, two immediate problems emerge, both of which are superficial. One is that unlike the preceding examples, the age-specific implications of the later 1960s on party identification strength are less than obvious. Certainly some could be ginned up if necessary, but only with a degree of mental effort which renders them less compelling.

The other problem is that in talking of age-impact functions for period effects, we have been talking of a hypothetical ideal assessment, "if the truth were known." Whether the truth is knowable is another question, and the basic indeterminacy in cohort inference suggests that it is

not. In other words, if we were to take our party identification data from the post-1964 period to estimate such an
impact function empirically, we would be subject to the
challenge that a difference in response between young and
old might not be period-effect-related so much as a standard
life-cycle shift.

In response to such a challenge, our hand is by now
uncommonly strong. For one thing, our clear results from the
steady-state period lead us to imagine quite shamelessly that
we know something about "standard life-cycle shifts," and
buttressing evidence from other times simply screws our
sense of plausibility up another notch or two. Furthermore,
the intrusion of the life-cycle concept in this context is in no
way confounding: in talking about age-impact functions, we
are dealing squarely with the interaction of period effects and
stages in the life cycle, and the chronological age index has
no third meaning here, particularly if we remove cohorts
entering the scene after the onset of the period effects. It is
true that we are still short of proof, because it is always
possible that the period itself has turned all "standard" pure
life-cycle process parameters upside down. But such a
possibility at least shifts the burden of proof to the
challenger.

The lack of obvious age-specific implications of the party
identification strength component in the late 1960s is in one
sense a virtue, since it is probably a limited minority of all
the attributes that may engage the attention of cohort
analysts in coming decades which have age-specific implications as clear as those for our draft and social security
examples. Thus we can enjoy dealing with a rather more
general case.

In an inventive paper, Carlsson and Karlsson (1970) have
reviewed a fair range of evidence from both Sweden and the
United States supporting what they call a "fixation model"
of cohort change. In a nutshell, this model rests on the
hypothesis that proneness to change declines progressively

with age. Translated to our current vocabulary, such a model would suggest that in the absence of substance-specific implications to the contrary, the most plausible age-impact function to expect is not a rectangular one, but rather one which slopes downward with age: event impact is maximal among the young, moderate among the middle-aged, and minimal among the old.

This is, of course, exactly what even rudimentary analysis of the impact of period effects on the strength component since 1964 shows, and the patterns are writ so large that almost every cohort analyst of party identification has commented upon them. Under the pressures of the later 1960s, party loyalty has evaporated most rapidly among the young, more modestly among the middle-aged, and least for the old.

Figure 6 provides a first view of this effect. It is a crude and provisional view in several sense, although it mimics the kind of data assemblies which have produced the preceding conclusions among those inspecting this variable in the later period. It has been constructed in the following manner. As Figure 3 testifies, pyramiding the vast amount of data from the steady-state period produces an empirical age-strength relationship which is already smooth enough even by fine cohort that it fairly pleads to have the last steps of smoothing taken. This I naturally have done. It is a far more arbitrary task to smooth the small-sample raggedness of this relationship where any later single study is concerned. However, in 1974 three studies were taken over a span barely exceeding six months. When these are combined, there is enough coherence that a parallel smooth curve for 1974 can be devised without doing too much violence to the raw data. Figure 6 simply represents the difference between these smooth curves.

The figure is crude in part because it deals only with endpoint calculations, and fails to address at all whatever dynamics may have intervened between. Thus it mirrors no

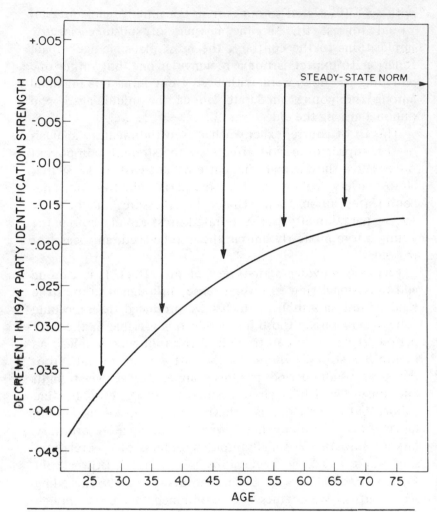

Figure 6: ACCUMULATED IMPACT OF PERIOD EFFECTS ON PARTY
IDENTIFICATION STRENGTH BETWEEN 1965 AND 1974, BY AGE

more than an impact as it has cumulated over a lengthy period of time. Moreover, it is a "cohort" description only in a very limited sense. It does not, for example, purport to gauge even the cumulative impact of the period on any specific birth cohort. Instead, it simply says that young people in 1974 were far weaker in their identifications than were cohorts of the steady-state period *at a corresponding age*.

There is nothing particularly wrong with this information, providing its limits are understood. However, it does not take much thought to realize that such a data assembly tends to exaggerate artificially any trend toward declining impact with age, as it might be measured by tracking the same birth cohorts over time.

Therefore it is worth bringing all of our post-1965 data to bear on the question of the internal dynamics of change by birth cohort that have marked this period, to get beneath the surface of Figure 6. However, this is easier said than done, for we do not get very far beneath the surface before we find ourselves rather badly tangled on the reefs of sampling error. Ideally, we should like to keep cohorts very finely divided over a high density of observation times, in order to track these cohort-specific impacts. However, such a tactic would presuppose that we had individual samples an order of magnitude or more larger than those we possess. Without extremely large samples, sampling "noise" rises to such a crescendo that it is difficult to make any assessments whatever, if time is kept finely divided both "horizontally" (passage of real time) and "vertically" up the cohort age ladder.

It turns out, however, that we cannot even afford the luxury of deciding to collapse along one of these time dimensions while retaining fine distinctions on the other. We must collapse cases along both dimensions to arrive at case numbers maintaining much clarity of signal. This is a different situation than that which we encountered in Chapter 3, where we maintained fine (three-year) cohort divisions and counted on linear estimates of cohort change over time to solve problems of sampling irregularities from particular sample to particular sample. In that instance, there was abundant warrant to expect at least approximately linear time-change effects associated with gradual aging. But now we are dealing with what we know to be period effects, with all of the irregularities of jolts and shocks that such a concept seems to entail. Indeed, one of the most fascinating questions to be asked is whether the impacts have registered as rather discrete pulsations over this period, or as a steadier (linear) pressure; and we cannot ask such a question if we use procedures which will only recognize linear change as a signal amid the noise.

In this regard, it is important to recognize that figures like 1 or 5 risk being quite deceptive. With one exception, just after the first downturn, the decline in aggregate strength has been remarkably linear in the total sample, suggesting either a model of steady pressure over time or a model of a more discrete jolt whose effects only gradually penetrate through the population as time passes. However, a major component of the steadiness of the decline is the fact that one set of extreme cases on the strength measure—new voters after 1965—have risen from 0 percent of the electorate at the moment of downturn to nearly one-third of the electorate as of 1975. The rate of infusion has had all the steady majesty of most demographic forms of change, and does a lot toward steepening and smoothing the apparent trend. Yet if we are to trace cohorts over time from 1965 onward, this infusion is out of our field of view entirely.

With such considerations in mind, I have been willing to throw away almost all cohort discrimination in order to maintain as much discrimination by time of observation as possible. The subsequent analyses refer to an extremely gross cutting into three cohorts from the pre-1965 electorate, partitioned to achieve a reasonable balance of cases, particularly in the early stages of the period where case numbers are weakest. These include the cohorts with birth years from 1928 to 1943, all of whom were eligible to vote in 1964; the cohort from 1912 to 1927, who ranged from thirty-eight years of age to sixty-three over the course of this period; and the somewhat broader (but progressively shrinking) cohort of those born between 1884 and 1911.

Even with this heroic amount of cohort collapsing, time traces remain suspiciously ragged without some collapsing as well of closely adjacent studies, much as we have already used in figures like 5. And this tactic is not available to us for the early portion of the period, when studies were too sparsely distributed in time to make such combination palatable.

A good example of the problems still caused by weak case numbers involves the behavior of the oldest cohort in the 1966-1968 period. The 1966 study was the smallest in the whole period, and has no near temporal neighbors with which it may be combined. In that year, all three cohorts show precipitous declines in identification strength, including the oldest cohort, which we might have expected on other grounds to have been most insulated from the impact. In the 1968 study, also limited in size and isolated in time, the two younger cohorts remain near their new-found lows, but the value for the old rebounds not only back to the steady-state norm for a group of its age composition, but actually beyond that norm, very much as though nothing whatever had happened in 1966. In fact, although after 1968 strength declines progressively among the old, it is a full six years and numerous studies before one again finds a value for the oldest cohort as low as that registered in 1966.

It is thus extremely tempting to regard the 1966 value for the oldest cohort as no more than a particularly aberrant sampling bounce. After all, the cases involved are few (N of 386), and the difference seems within reasonable sampling range, although even the latter judgment must remain muddy in this context.[7] Moreover, if we see this as a stray value which would not have been replicated in another study at the same time, the peculiar bend in the total-sample trend in 1966 and 1968 largely is not completely straightens out (see Figure 5), and the SRC-CPS data move into slightly greater harmony with the Gallup data for the same period. Finally, if we seek to erase the anomaly by combining 1966 and 1968 data for the oldest cohort exceptionally, as we do in Figure 7, the resulting time trace for that cohort over the whole period is delightfully smooth without further editorial intrusion.

However, it would be quite possible to trust this 1966 data point and give it a substantive interpretation. Such an interpretation would argue that the old were responding in 1966 to exactly the same events as were registering in the two younger cohorts. What is different is that the imprint of those events was more or less permanent for the younger people, and utterly transient for the old. There is no way to choose between these interpretations without recourse to other sources, and we have left the anomaly in Figure 8. The reader may choose, but unfortunately the conceptual stakes involved in the choice are rather high.

Figure 7 represents my optimal solution for the time traces for these three cohorts between 1965 and 1975 if apparent sampling irregularities are to be minimized while keeping the cross-time discrimination of observation times at a reasonably sharp level.[8] Figure 7 is annotated so that rough case numbers can be kept in mind. These numbers are distinctly at their weakest where the single Fall 1975, study is concerned, and this study is left uncombined chiefly because of the high interest that attaches to the "latest" figures. The conservative reader may wish largely to discount these final values.

In some respects, Figure 7 is disappointing. Enough irregularity remains present, some of it due to sampling error, that about the single "safe" conclusion to be drawn, particularly if one pays attention to the points best fortified with cases, is that all three cohorts have shown declines during this period, a fact which we already knew. Moreover, although we retained three gross cohorts deliberately to see whether the middle-aged were also middling between young and old in other key process parameters like response

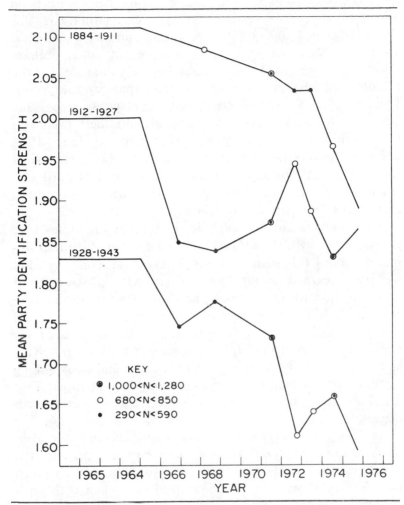

Figure 7: CHANGES IN PARTY IDENTIFICATION STRENGTH SINCE 1964,
BY GROSS COHORT

amplitude or response lag, it is not abundantly apparent from
Figure 7 that this is the case. Although the middle-aged have
shown very little decline since the initial shock prior to 1966,
their response to that first shock was seemingly more
vigorous than among those either older or younger. This is

quite contrary to expectation, although the case numbers on which the 1966 observation rests are very limited (423 for the middle-aged, and 396 for the young), and we would need samples at least half again as big showing the same configuration before we could say with any normal assurance that the middle-aged response was greater than that for the young. Figure 7 *does* appear to argue that the response among the elderly has been weaker and lagged, although even this conclusion can be called into question if the combined 1966 and 1968 points are broken apart for that cohort, as we shall see shortly. All told, we are close to losing this particular battle with sampling error, particularly where the crucial early half of the period is concerned.

There is one further analytic refinement on these three gross cohorts which adds at least marginally to our information about this period. Figure 7 takes no account of what we have learned about "normal" growth in strength of partisanship with aging from our dissections of the steady-state period. If these rates of growth were constant at all ages, we could safely ignore them in the current analysis. However, we have found that these growth rates are relatively large for the young, moderate in middle age, and weak among the elderly. It is natural to wonder what would happen if we laid the cohort traces from this period against such growth expectations.

At least two observations, one empirical and one conceptual, must be made by way of preface. Empirically it is worth noting, in clear reminiscence from earlier chapters, that in any short time the magnitudes of change through growth are really quite small by comparison with the magnitudes of change tied up in the period-borne decline. More especially, the *differences* in growth rate expected from young to old are smaller yet, and we should hardly expect any insertion of them as expectations to create radical change in the picture created by Figure 7.

It is also fair to ask whether conceptually such growth

expectations should be taken into account at all after 1964. Any such gradual "normal" growth would seem likely to be the very first casualty of the onset of strong forces dampening feelings of partisan loyalty. Of course, in one sense such an argument is impeccable: there has been no growth of party strength in any of our cohorts over this period. However, there are two ways to conceptualize the period of decline, and there is no way the data can be used to choose between them. According to one view, whatever happened in 1965 totally restructured the game: while a persistent tendency toward growth must be posited to understand age change in the preceding twenty years or more, the game changed as of 1965 and these life-cycle increments have retreated to zero; the aggregate declines which we observe are the register of pure forces associated with period effects. According to the other view, the same forces toward growth are present after 1965 as before, but what we witness as declines are the resultant of an upward growth force and a still stronger downward period effect.

I do not care to choose between these alternatives. But there is no reason why we should not heuristically follow the second possibility, having implicitly examined the first in Figure 7. Therefore we have rearranged the data to estimate the "pure" impact of period forces on the assumption that they are acting contrapuntally against a continuing trend toward growth. This is done by calculating an expected rate of growth for cohorts of each of our three age mixes over each duration or subperiod bounded by observations in Figure 7. Then to the empirically observed initial value for the cohort at the beginning of the period, a growth increment proportional to the duration of the subperiod is added to form an expectation for the value to be shown by the cohort at the end of the period. The measure of the accumulated impact of period forces for the particular subperiod and cohort in question is the difference between the observed value and the expectation.

This procedure is very straightforward with one exception. While we have firm and abundant estimates of differential growth rates for the steady-state period, the impact of period effects after 1965 has forced the mean values of many of our cohorts into ranges of the identification strength variable not seen before. If fifty-year-olds in 1974 show mean values comparable to those shown by twenty-one-year-olds in the earlier period, should we expect their growth rates in 1974 (period depressants aside) to be the rapid ones shown by earlier twenty-one-year-olds starting from the same base; or do we instead imagine that they are merely the sluggish ones shown by fifty-year-olds before 1965?

This is obviously a cardinal question conceptually, as well as for our immediate computational needs. It is a question that future investigators, profiting from still more history passed before us, may be able to address quite firmly. However, we must make a more tentative assumption. Our expectations will be formed on the supposition that differential growth rates are specific to chronological ages, rather than to the absolute starting-point on the scale. I feel there are two reasons for such a choice. One is that while relevant data from such as middle-aged party changers or immigrants are very fragmentary at best, they all support such an assumption in preference to its rival. They could easily be overturned by more incisive data, but we shall depend on them now for they are all we have. Secondly, it is true that an assumption linking growth rates directly to age, rather than starting-point, is in the immediate context the more conservative of the two assumptions, in the sense of minimizing our rearrangements of the raw data. To hitch growth rates to starting-points would create expectations of quite breathtaking age gains for younger people in the current period.

When such further computations are performed, we find data of the sort depicted in Figure 8. Within each subperiod bounded by observations, we know nothing of the differential distribution of impacts by time. We simply know what impact has accumulated as of the end of the period, and we then presume it to have been rectangularly distributed across the interval of nonmeasurement, for purposes of graphing. The unshaded rectangles rising above the zero-line of expected growth are in one sense anomalies, being cases in which the cohort value at the end of the measurement subperiod actually exceed what would have been predicted on the basis of growth expectations alone. Fortunately, these "rebounds" are few and usually quite small. We have said enough earlier about the high sampling variability surrounding all of these estimates that small departures from growth expectations are of absolutely no interest. And the most noteworthy case of excess in Figure 8 is the rebound of the old in the second (1966-1968) time phase, which we had obscured for purposes of Figure 7 by combining adjacent observations.

If we focus our attention upon the major departures from growth expectations in Figure 8, we see one distinct pattern. Each cohort appears to have been struck by two discrete shocks, with a period of relative quiescence between these shocks (1967-1968 for all cohorts, and longer for the older two). The brunt of the second shock registers in the period from late 1971 to late 1972 for the young; from late 1972 to mid-1973 for the middle-aged, with further spillover to late 1974; and from late 1973 through 1974 and, if we were to trust the small 1975 sample, on through much of 1975. This is exactly the kind of progressive rippling of the impact from young through the middle-aged to the old that we had more or less expected in advance.

The first shock appears, however, to have had effects "across the board" in terms of age, at least if we trust the 1966 data point for the old. Or alternatively, if we do not trust that point, the first shock registered almost not at all on the old (cf. Figure 7). Yet we cannot be sure that there was no comparable "ripple" involved in the first shock. The later

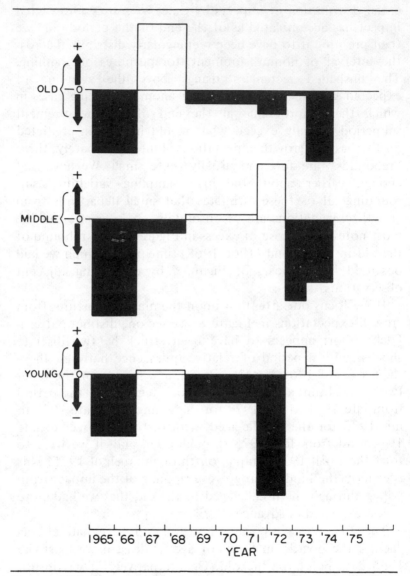

Figure 8: IMPACTS ON PARTY IDENTIFICATION STRENGTH IN PERIODS
SINCE 1964, BY GROSS COHORT

shock registered first upon the young at some time prior to late 1972, and had impacted on the old at least prior to late 1974. Hence the whole rippling process need not have spanned as much as twenty-four months. Where the first shock is concerned, we have evidence that the effects began to register very soon after the beginning of the first measurement period in January-February, 1965. Then there is no measurement for twenty months, and Figure 8 assumes that the impact accumulated after this twenty-month period had been rectangularly distributed for all three cohorts over the period. It is possible that this gross spacing of observations in the early period conceals a "ripple" very much like that of the later period, when more frequent observations are available to make it plain.

It should be made clear that at this point we are treating these data quite heuristically for the moment, being unable to demand firmer proof from our limited case numbers. However, the kind of two-shock model strongly suggested by Figure 8 has a number of additional facts to recommend it. For one thing, it is worth emphasizing that the two-shock impression created by Figure 8 is far more dependent on the fact that the data are reformatted by comparison with Figure 7 than it is on the fact that Figure 8 takes account of growth expectations, while Figure 7 does not. It is true that taking account of growth expectations does seem to add a final dollop of clarification to the two-shock impression, mainly by reducing some small "rebounds" in Figure 7 to little more than would be expected from normal growth in a time of quiescence where period effects are concerned. But the Figure 8 data are only very marginally changed over those in Figure 7 as a result of taking those growth expectations into account; and the two-shock sequence can clearly be read in Figure 7, although the Figure 8 format helps to heighten the visual impression.

More importantly, there is external evidence supporting a two-shock sequence. Glenn (1972), writing from Gallup materials covering the period up through 1971 and perhaps early 1972, was intrigued by the evidence that after an initial shock depressing partisanship from mid-1965 to mid-1967, there seemed to be a partial rebound up through 1971. He localizes the lion's share of the early decline in party loyalties within the South. But he also notes (pp. 504-505) that most of the later "rebound" to partisanship that he saw in his 1971 data also occurred within the South; it was the smaller margin of partisan decline beginning in 1965-1967 *outside* the South that seemed to persist to the end of his observations. What Glenn was looking at as a rebound is clearly visible in the Gallup trend which shows a leveling, 1967-1969, and an upward scallop thereafter to 1972, in figures like 1 and 4. The more differentiated SRC-CPS identification strength measure on the total electorate shows no comparable upward scallop, although there is a breath of a reversal in the late 1960s. However, the Gallup scallop coincides perfectly with the period of near-quiescence from 1967 to 1971 that is highlighted by the SRC-CPS data in Figure 8. And it is this intervening period of quiescence or rebound that intervenes to create an impression of two quite distinct shocks to the strength of party identification over the total period.

Finally, if it could be shown that the two apparent sags in strength of partisanship had shown different patterns within the two major parties, we would have further prima facie evidence that the response in the two cases was to qualitatively different "events," and hence that different shocks were involved. According to conventional wisdom, the initial decline after 1965 hurt the Democrats disproportionately, whereas the later shock in 1972 and beyond has chiefly eroded the loyalties of Republicans. This conventional wisdom has some measure of truth to it, as it turns out, although I hesitate to cite it authoritatively because some of the evidence pointed to is in my opinion spurious.

The matter becomes somewhat complex, and we shall not

delve into it in any detail here. Complexities arise because as soon as we observe change in party identification strength within the sets of Democrats and Republicans, we must multiply our indicators, and these indicators need not covary neatly over time. This is so because in our normal strength measure, pure independents and apoliticals are scored at the low extreme of partisanship. However, when we examine the distribution of strength within each party, this tail of the distribution drops off, since it is not assignable to either party. Thus we arrive at two measures of intra-party strength, one for each party. But these two measures are not adequate to describe the situation, since there may have been a net imbalance of flows into the pure independent category between the parties. To reflect this, we must add a third indicator, such as the ratio of identifiers and leaners in the two camps. If within a given period the main flow across the party identification distribution has been a drain from "leaning Democrats" to independents, then the intra-party strength of the Democrats will increase at the very same time that its numerical strength relative to the Republicans is decreasing. I have examined all of these patterns, and they are quite coherent over time at the total-sample level; but a full description would involve too long a detour for our current argument.

Suffice it to say that the main ground for the conclusion that the shock to partisanship registering after 1965 chiefly bore on the Democrats is the simple fact that self-reported Democrats in the total electorate were notably fewer in proportion to Republicans by 1966 or 1968 than they had been in 1964. This is not a very adequate analysis. We shall see in the next chapter that the relative balance of Democrats and Republicans shifts up and down in response to short-term fortunes of the two parties. This oscillation, although much more restricted than swings in the national vote itself, is best seen as reflecting the fact that some very limited fraction of respondents (and they can readily be identified as the least politically involved) responds more to these items as a statement of current vote leanings than of a more generalized and abiding sense of party belonging (presumably because they lack any such sense). It is not surprising that the amplitude of this oscillation around its fairly constant mean is visibly sharper for the Gallup partisanship item than for the SRC-CPS measure of party identification, given the wordings of the two questions (see Chapter 3). But even with the more stable SRC-CPS measure, oscillations of ±1-2 percent in the proportion of Democrats among all identifiers are endemic in the record, nicely correlating with independent information as to short-term party fortunes. And in occasional extremes, these oscillations reach a magnitude of ±5 percent.

There have been at least two such extremes in the past thirty years. One surrounded the 1956 landslide victory of Eisenhower for his second term; and the second surrounded the 1964 landslide victory of Lyndon Johnson. In both cases, the short-term oscillation in partisanship was visible well before the election, and had subsided within twelve months after the election. Even the magnitudes of these two oscillations are neatly comparable, and if one had used the 1955-1958 sequence to predict what would happen to the pre-Democratic swing of 1963-1964 as 1965 and 1966 passed, the size of the Democratic subsidence in that critical period would have been predicted almost to perfection, without the need to deal in uncommon events whatever.

Hence the main evidence adduced to demonstrate that the Democrats were disproportionately the losers in the face of the 1965-1966 shock seems quite misguided. In fact, if we look at the intra-party loyalty strength for Democrats and Republicans over the whole period from 1960 to 1975, we find that *both* parties show one interval of precipitous drop, with only minor gains and slides elsewhere in the record. This one crisp fall lies between the 1965 and 1966 observation for the Democrats, and between 1965 and 1968 for the Republicans. What is more, the magnitude of the drop in this indicator is if anything slightly *greater* among Republicans than among Democrats; and if we limit our attention to the pre-1965 electorate, then the more extended drop among Republicans is two to three times greater than that for the Democrats, whose slide had stopped abruptly in 1966. This was not because the Republicans were gaining new weak adherents in large numbers, for they were not.

Therefore there is powerful evidence that the 1965-1966 shock was quite discrete in time, and that it had a major impact on partisans of both stripes. If we are willing to say that there is some truth in the judgment that the Democrats were the greater losers by some small margin in the response to 1965-1966, it is chiefly because the infusion of new voters in the 1964-1968 period favored the Democrats enough that their subsidence after the high tide of 1964 should have enjoyed more cushioning than it shows. Indeed, it is only when one looks at the complex of patterns within the pre-1965 electorate that one can reliably conclude that the Democrats were in fact marginally the greater losers from the episodes involved. It remains important diagnostically, however, that the impact on Republicans was clear as well.

The second shock, which Figure 8 would date as having its effects starting in 1972, is in some respects more obscure, and in some respects less obscure, than its predecessor. It is more obscure in that it seems more complex and long-drawn-out in its phasing, and less well described as a highly-localized "shock." To some degree, as noted earlier, this difference in apparent localization may be no more than a simple artifact of the greater density of observations in the second period. To some degree, too, the phasing may demand descriptions in terms of a ripple from young to old. However, when one examines the differential party patterns in the same vein we have discussed them for 1965-1966, the sense of complexity is enhanced. In particular, the party patterns surrounding the first phase of this second shock (prior to early 1973, and registering most heavily in the youngest third of the pre-1965 electorate) do not seem to fit at all well with the party patterns characterizing the remainder of the period, up through 1975. What is less obscure about this period is that in these later stages, the Republicans have suffered more sharply than the Democrats, and by a clearer margin than was true in the reverse direction in 1965-1966. The losers at the outset of the period (essentially, 1972) were equally clearly the Democrats.

Now 1972 was another landslide in the national presidential vote, this time favoring the Republicans. If I failed to mention it in the same breath as the 1956 and 1964 landslides in discussing short-term oscillations in statements of partisanship, it is not because no parallel oscillation is visible in that year. It is visible, and shows just about the same hump form as one sees in connection with the two earlier landslides. But it does not seem to rank in the same category because its amplitude is quite muffled by comparison with the earlier instances. Moreover, unlike those instances, the hump was accompanied both fore and aft by a continuing net decline in partisan loyalties. To some degree the net Democratic losses moving up to the 1972 election, and the net Republican losses as it receded in time, undoubtedly deserve to be conceptualized as part of an old and familiar rhythm. But the accompaniment of a new round of erosion in party loyalty is something different.

After 1972 the relative numerical strength of the Republicans dwindles quite markedly. Part of this is normal subsidence after the 1972 high tide. An additional part reflects the fact that the "exchange rate" between the dying elderly and the incoming young has a partisan imbalance favoring the Democrats by a wide margin. If one restricts the focus to the pre-1965 electorate, the apparent loss in relative Republican strength from 1972 to 1975 is cut about in half. Nonetheless, there is a significant loss to the Republicans even in that stratum of the electorate, and one that does not appear to be entirely interpretable as normal subsidence.

Moreover, while the intra-party strength among the Democrats remains essentially constant after 1972, the same term
is declining for Republicans, especially in the older, pre-1965
segment of the Republican electorate. The decline is fairly
limited relative to the major plunge of the same term for the
Republicans after 1965, but it remains unmistakable.

Identifying the Two Shocks. Earlier in this chapter, after
pains had been taken to localize the onset of "period effects"
to a rather narrow span of time between June and October of
1965, the question as to what real-world events catalyzed
those unusual responses was sidestepped. But it was only
intended to be postponed until we had had a chance to
review the more detailed ebb and flow of the party
identification strength responses over the whole period. This
reconnaissance has suggested that there are at least two
distinct shocks to be identified.

The first of these two intruded abruptly in 1965 but had
some reverberations at least until 1968 and perhaps 1970.
This shock was, in terms of the magnitude of the response,
quite clearly the sharper of the two. It also had what was
more nearly an "across-the-board" quality. It impacted on
partisans of both camps, although marginally more strongly
among Democrats. And by one reading of the data at least
(Figure 8), it impacted very generally on citizens of all ages.
The subsequent "natural history" of the impact was quite
different by age. It decayed with lightning speed among the
older cohorts, in their fifties and beyond at the time of
impact. For those of more middling age (thirty-eight through
fifty-four at the time of impact) there was also a visible
rebound, although it worked itself out at a slower pace over
the years from 1968 to 1972. There was virtually no rebound
at all among those who were still younger, although in the
electorate at the time of impact. For this cohort the
depressive imprint has appeared permanent. The second
shock (or shocks) was smaller, and at least in its later phases
more limited to older Republicans.

What events constituted these shocks? For most trend lines of variables that are event-dependent, and which show sudden large displacements at particular points in time, it is customary to review events on the historical record in the period immediately preceding the displacement, and to sort out one or two that seem to have common-sense implications for disrupting the trend in the direction observed, and assigning them as "causes." We cannot particularly improve on such a rather hapless, post hoc procedure here. However, it is worth doing so only in a guarded fashion, especially in this particular case.

The requirements of the mass media industry are such that events are always with us; and although some events as amplified and disseminated through that industry are obviously more important than others, many factors conspire to create the impression that events are rather rectangularly distributed across time. Daily newspapers, weekly news-magazines, and annual summaries of national events are not given to saying that "not much happened" in this particular day, or week, or year. Thus for any jag in a trend we are rarely wanting for candidate causes, although a little skepticism often can produce counter-events from the same pool which, had the trend turned the other way, could with equal facility be extracted as "causes."

In the special case of party identification strength, however, we are not free to pick any contemporaneous event as a cause, without taking cognizance of the fact that we need to find events that can objectively be viewed as epochal in their importance. After all, the whole period from 1944 to 1975 has been strewn with events, many of them major, and some of which could be fashioned, in a common-sense manner, into reasons why the American public might have suffered disenchantment with one or both of the major parties. Yet none of these important events appears to have jarred these loyalties perceptibly over more than two decades; and then suddenly they are jarred in dramatic fashion. To retain any plausibility at·all, we cannot deal in the common run of even dramatic, major events.

Despite this caution, I am not uncomfortable in presuming that the sequence of events known as Watergate had a prime role in the post-1972 phase of the second shock. Probably more disastrous "firsts" went onto the record of the American presidency within an eighteen-month span than had occurred since the time when the Republic was very young. Some two or three earlier administrations had suffered major and perhaps even epochal taints of corruption, which led to the successful prosecution of as many as two or three more or less prominent political or administrative personalities. But none of these earlier events, however important they were in their time, involved anything like the number of high-level prosecutions stemming from the Watergate revelations, and often for at least semi-independent acts of unlawfulness. For example, the disclosures precipitating the resignation of Vice President Agnew, an uncommonly visible and vociferous party spokesman for a number of years, appeared to have been quite independent of the mainstream of Watergate abuses. And, of course, the ultimate presidential resignation in disgrace, along with acceptance of executive pardon, was historically unprecedented.

Thus the epochal status of Watergate seems scarcely problematic. Moreover, its common-sense impact meshes neatly with the empirical observations, which show disproportionate disillusion among Republicans at their political party. The clear "ripple" effect from middle-aged to older Republicans over this period may well reflect nothing more than differential willingness to accept the evidence as it developed and tightened over the eighteen months during which the revelations were evolving.

But the very neatness of the fit in the case of the second shock merely underscores the peculiarity of the first shock, which if anything appears to have been stronger, more sudden, and less party-specific (although with some special force, perhaps, upon southern Democrats).

I will confess that I returned to the history of the spring and summer of 1965 with a large measure of skepticism that events which would satisfy me as epochal could be discerned. Of course I knew that the twin spurs of the massive discontent of the later 1960s—Vietnam and the racial issue—were already centers of bitter controversy as of that year. Indeed, I knew that this critical six-month period exactly coincided with the dramatic and unexpected expansion of the Vietnam War, but there were ample grounds to doubt that these events could be very convincingly seen as responsible for the observed impact. And my recollection of the ebbs and flows of racial strife was that it had, of course, started much earlier, had hit a marked crescendo well before the spring of 1965, and had sustained that crescendo until very well beyond the end of 1966. While I was assured that one could find incidents of major racial violence within that six- or eight-month period, including undoubtedly some important ones, I assumed that a comparable set could be found for periods of the same duration two years before and three or more years after.

I will also confess that I came away from my review of events in and around the period from February, 1965, to September, 1965, feeling somewhat mollified. Over this precise period there was a density of events surrounding both Vietnam and race relations which was indeed almost overwhelming, and which I suspect might be shown more objectively to have stood out on the record even against the backdrop of a generally troubled time.

Let me speak first to Vietnam, where the timing of events relative to the observed impact approaches perfection. Between about the second week of February and early fall of 1965 was the period of most rapid mobilization and escalation of the American effort in Vietnam. It is the period of the first sharp threats, the first use of B-52 bombers, the first bombings of Hanoi, the first unvarnished commission of American ground troops to combat, and particularly in the summer of 1965, the rapid expansion of the draft. Other mobilizations and escalations were to follow for a half-dozen years; but after the first effort they became in some degree only more of the same.

The rapid mobilization was unexpected among the citizenry, but this fact in itself would in no sense distinguish it from the outbreak of the Korean War, which was even less foreseen. What distinguished Vietnam from Korea was a segment of opinion which had become much more chary of "brushfire wars," especially on the Asian landmass, and which had construed a major axis of the 1964 presidential campaign to be a debate between a challenger advocating the vigorous expansion of the Vietnam commitment, and an incumbent who advocated a more moderate course of limited participation. This segment of opinion perceived, moreover, that not only had the advocate of moderation won the election, but he had won by a nearly unprecedented landslide. Therefore when Lyndon Johnson, scarcely two weeks after his inauguration, began to signal that the country was poised on the brink of an expansion of the war at least of the proportions advocated by the defeated candidate, the sense of betrayal in this segment of opinion was almost overwhelming, a sense scarcely alleviated by the march of events into the summer and fall, or rumors that the expansion planning had already been underway in the midst of the campaign debate.

This is a picture of a *segment* of opinion. Within that segment, largely if not completely confined to college campuses, the sense of rage was extreme. Over a period of thirty years in this environment, I do not remember even a vague equal, with the possible exception of Watergate. If one demands harder "behavioral" indicators of the magnitude of the dismay, they are present in the teach-ins and related disturbances that began in March, 1965, and spread rapidly in the autumn of the year across the nation's major universities.

There is no doubt that this sequence of events in the spring and summer of 1965 moved some habitual Democrats into a position of thorough disenchantment with their party. Live bodies can be produced who will attest to that. The real question, however, is one of magnitude, and here all the available evidence suggests that the number of outraged persons was so limited that any nationwide, aggregate decline in party strength produced as a result would have been almost invisible, given the usual margin of uncertainty provided by sampling error.

If we look to data provided by the total electorate in this microperiod, the Vietnam shock was of minor significance. It is true that the public rating of Lyndon Johnson's performance as president dropped steadily by Gallup poll indicators from the time of his first inauguration after the Kennedy assassination to the period after his discouraged announcement in the spring of 1968 that he would not run again. But it is also true that such a decline of one extent or duration or another, has followed the inauguration of every president since appropriate records have been kept (Mueller, 1970). It is also true that the decline in Johnson's popularity was more precipitous and extended than most. Yet it is true at the same time that this rate of decline was not uncommonly steep in 1965, and that indeed 1965 sets itself apart from 1964, 1966, 1967 and 1968 in that there was no uncommon collapse of popularity in the middle of the year.

Still more incisive evidence is provided by public reactions to the Vietnam War, and more particularly, public ratings of Johnson's handling of the Vietnam situation. If college feelings of betrayal had enjoyed more resonance than the minority of a small minority, then both of these indicators should show a major drop between February and October, 1965. They do not. Public enthusiasm about the war actually increased in tune with the mobilization, and reached its all-time peak late in the fall of 1965 (Mueller, 1971: 364). It was not until 1967 and 1968 that a visible "war-weariness" began to trouble the population. Unfortunately, the most relevant indicator—ratings of Johnson's handling of the war—was not begun in standard form apparently until about July, 1965. But even that indicator is moving upward over what measurements are available in the critical period.[9]

In short, then, Vietnam must have made some contribution to the sudden decline in party loyalties in this brief period. Nonetheless, the contribution was surely limited in magnitude.

Where racial turmoil is concerned, the mid-1960s had no monopoly, nor is there the same neatness of timing that matches the Vietnam mobilization with the sudden decline of party loyalties. But an impressionistic review of events within the February-October period in 1965, along with still sketchier reviews of the whole 1963-1968 period, is enough to convince me that the six months from March to August of that year had a density of major conflicts which may well be objectively unmatched since World War II. Certainly any list of major events in the civil rights movement would honor the historical significance of episodes such as the Montgomery bus sit-in or the sending of federal troops to Little Rock in the 1950s. Yet where the threat of overflowing violence between the races was concerned, these were relatively sedate affairs. If one were to restrict the list to major confrontations with violence present and threatening to run beyond all control, then Selma and Watts would surely rank among the four or five major events of the whole twenty-year period. The outbreak of police violence at Selma, Alabama, accompanied by vigilante murders, occurred in March, 1965, after having festered since January. Scarcely five months later, in August, the Watts ghetto went up in flames. In between lay a sprinkling of other violent and near-violent mass encounters, including Bogalusa, Louisiana, and stretching even into the North, with the Chicago march.

This compression of events in itself need not have much indisputable impact on the kinds of attitudes bound up in the strength of party loyalties, however profoundly unsettling the trend of history was to most Americans at the time. However, these further links are not entirely difficult to establish. Dependent upon one's persuasions in racial matters, this microperiod had a wealth of episodes calculated to produce a profound disenchantment with the whole political system.

For liberals, the period was laced with an astonishing sequence of acquittals and quashed indictments by southern juries and judges in a spate of civil rights murders. For conservatives, it was a period in which the federal courts and the Johnson Administration lost no opportunity to demonstrate a national resolve to enforce without delay the comparatively "radical" Civil Rights Act passed in July of 1964. In April, 1965, for example, the United States Commissioner of Education announced that all of the nation's 27,000 public school districts would be required to desegregate completely by September, 1967, with a "substantial start" as of September, 1965. This was a far faster timetable than the South had come to imagine, and the North was just beginning to realize that it also had no shelter from this form of enforced social change.

President Johnson himself, in a tense series of confrontations with Governor Wallace of Alabama, ordered federal troops into the state to protect the Selma marchers. Throughout the spring and summer his national speeches made relentlessly clear to the South that there was to be no escape from the implications of the Civil Rights Act. For a region that had waited a century for a recognizably "southern" president like Johnson, the sense of betrayal must have been every bit as keen as that experienced by the far smaller contingent of northern liberals who assumed that the nation had just made a hands-down choice in favor of a leadership cautious about the Vietnam commitment. For those less ideologically committed on either Vietnam or the race issue, the compounding of violent events both at home and abroad in the February-October period may well have led to an uneasy feeling that something must be dreadfully wrong with the national political leadership.

Such an account is, of course, post hoc. If it does not entirely explain why the nation's Republican identifiers showed a significant decline in feelings of party loyalty as the Democratic president seemed to betray first one trust and then another, it is true that the explosions of internal violence and foreign war marking 1965 were unsettling on a front which might well overflow conventional party lines. Moreover, such an account squares with the few known facts of the 1965 decline, including its mild epicenter among southern Democrats. It also squares with the Glenn (1972) reconstruction that a large initial sag among southern Democrats had been substantially restored by 1970 or 1971, whereas a smaller initial sag among Democrats outside the South still remained as of that date.

Thus both of the major shocks seem reasonably intelligible.[10] It is obvious there is no way the occurrence of the shocks could have been predicted in advance, and we are only beginning here the process of understanding what kind of shock is required and what happens in its wake. With only two examples of such shocks we cannot proceed very far; yet it is worth lingering over their causes as we have done, to supply fuel for future understanding when a still longer span of time has been observed with some care.

Long-Range Implications

Carlsson and Karlsson (1970) have suggested an interesting set of long-run implications that might be expected if their fixation model (proneness to change declining with age) pertained over a random sequence of shocks distributed through time. To my eye, the evidence from this period supports a fixation model, particularly if the field of view is expanded to include those under voting age at the time of these shocks. The age gradient involved is not magnificently steep, nor is it true that change-proneness goes all the way to zero among the old, as even Figure 6 attests. Moreover, it is at least possible that while the age-impact function was quite dramatic in the expected direction for the first shock, the Watergate shock was one with higher impact among the elderly. However all this may be, we shall not pursue the Carlsson-Karlsson implications here, in part simply because the record suggests that it is only very recently (relative to the past two generations) that uncommon "stimulus pressures" have intruded, thereby leaving too short a period for the evolution of those effects in clear form.

There are some other obvious implications of this period for the future, however. As several prior analysts have pointed out, aggregate levels of identification strength are likely to continue to decline for a considerable period into the future even without any further depressant events in the political system, simply because of the iron logic of population turnover, and the steady replacement of elderly partisans with young independents.

I have worked out a few crude projections to dramatize the strength of these continuing downward pressures on party loyalties in the nation. These projections are most definitely not intended as predictions, at least in the full-blown sense of the term. We do not know what new "period effects" lie ahead, and any reasonable projections proceed on the assumption of a new set of constancies which resemble those of the earlier steady-state period.

Nonetheless, such an exercise is not totally sterile. After all, we do know a great deal about the dynamics of population turnover, including the parameters of its most inevitable aspects, death and replacement. Fertility rates are the Achilles heel of population projections, but we do not even need special wisdom on that score if we do not try to look too far ahead. We are dealing with the *adult* population, rather than the total one; and the age mixture of the adult population is at the time of writing determined to within a

very narrow approximation (highly novel intrusions excluded) almost to the year 2000. We admittedly know less
about the dynamics of party identification strength, but it is
not as though we knew nothing at all. There is no reason why
we should not harness such relevant information to a
projection, less to commit ourselves to a prediction, than to
express the forces in the situation which other unforeseen
intrusions will either reinforce or be obliged to counter.

Figure 9 presents three such projections. The first, labelled
"No Change," is the simplest and perhaps the least realistic.
It assumes that each cohort in the electorate as of 1974 or
1975 has been imprinted with the strength value characteristic of it in those years, and maintains such a value
throughout the remainder of the life cycle. New entrants to
the electorate after 1975 continue to enter at the historically
low values being manifested by the new entrants of
1974-1975. Since these entry values had continued to plunge
during the first half of the 1970s, this trend was rounded off
to a low plateau in the later 1970s, and then left a constant
for further new entrants.

While such assumptions of "no change" are surely unreal-
istic, this projection has the virtue of showing in rather pure
form the forces which will be associated with predictable
demographic turnover over coming years. Other events may
act to reinforce or counter these downward pressures; but
whatever happens will be some resultant of unforeseeable
new inputs and downward pressures of this kind. As Figure 9
suggests, without other inputs, aggregate levels of identification strength would continue to decline at nearly the same
rate as in the 1965-1975 period until well beyond the year
2000, or until the population "homogenized" at the low
plateau (value of 1.10) of the new entrants of the mid-1970s.
Of course, assumptions concerning the values to assign new
entrants are among the most questionable of any that might
be made, and such assumptions begin to dominate the
solution in the later stage of any projection. Fortunately,

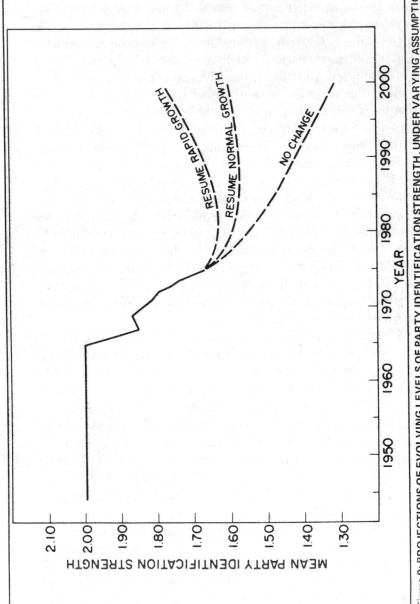

Figure 9: PROJECTIONS OF EVOLVING LEVELS OF PARTY IDENTIFICATION STRENGTH, UNDER VARYING ASSUMPTIONS

they have only limited weight for the early portions of the projection. In other words, if the future were left to pure demographic turnover, then as of 1975 we have scarcely witnessed a half of the total impact which the shocks of the 1965-1975 period will leave upon party loyalties in the electorate.

The first projection implicitly assumes that no further shocks intrude on identifications after 1975. If this were true, it might be more realistic to imagine that in lieu of such special pressures, the "normal" rates of growth characterizing the steady-state period would resume their visibility. Such growth rates for the steady-state period could be taken to be age-specific, or could be construed as specific to the starting point on the static curve of identification strength by age as observed in that period. Which assumption is chosen matters considerably. The events of the 1965-1975 period depressed the level of middle-aged party loyalties to absolute values formerly characteristic of the very young. If these period pressures are relaxed, do the middle-aged resume growth rates characteristic of the middle-aged in the earlier period, or do they show the rapid growth rates of the earlier young?

Earlier in this chapter, I have already noted my distinct preference for the "age-specific" hypothesis, although the future should provide an interesting critical test. This is therefore what is considered, for purposes of Figure 9, to be "normal," where growth rates are concerned. As we see, the disappearance of special period pressures on party loyalties after 1975 would mainly serve (even taking the downward demographic pressures into account) to leave the system at a new plateau, parallel to that for the steady-state period, but far lower. Whether this would actually be a new stable equilibrium, or merely a low from which a slow return to higher levels would be launched, depends of course on whether new entry values remained at their 1975 levels or began to drift back up toward their earlier characteristic values. The projection shown assumes some modest movement toward such a restoration.

The more lavish growth assumptions in the third projection takes growth rates to be specific to their absolute
starting point. It is of interest that even with this extravagant
assumption, only a modest fraction of the original decline
would be recouped even after nearly a generation.

To reiterate, all of these projections assume an intermediate future in which no further special shocks are
sustained, and that all the impact of past shocks has already
registered as of 1975 (save among those near entry into the
system). Quite naturally, further shocks may intrude. It is a
moot point whether the population would be less sensitive to
further depressant shocks of the same kind because of recent
experience; or would be more highly sensitized, such that less
portentous events could touch off further marked declines.
Nor should we forget the possibility that some new shock
might act in the opposing direction, to strengthen party
feelings beyond the normal growth rate. None such have been
witnessed, within the recorded history of these matters, but
they surely cannot be ruled out. Furthermore, if the shocks
which have led to weakened enthusiasm about party attachments have generally been national disasters, this need not
mean that shocks reinforcing partisanship should only be
sought among the set of potential national triumphs. Indeed,
perhaps the most obvious scenario for a shock stimulating
partisanship would be events or a period of deep national
cleavage, like the approach to the Civil War, in which the
major parties fell into clear opposition on an issue or issues of
vital moment to an emotionally-divided electorate.

Conclusion

Over the course of this chapter we have attempted a closer
scrutiny of the "period effects" since 1965, against the
backdrop of the preceding steady-state era, where the
strength of party identification is concerned. Some of the
story of this period, which may well not have ended, can be

more incisively reconstructed from disaggregations of the data not available to us in our large cohort data file. Nonetheless, we have attempted to address the timing of these period impacts, their apparent causes and likely futures, and most specifically, the distribution of these impacts by age cohort.

For the cohort analyst interested in other subject matters, perhaps the major lesson to be drawn is that the strength component of party identification adds to the rapidly-growing list of instances in which there are marked inter-actions between apparent period impacts and the chrono-logical age at which they are experienced. While the exact nature of these interactions cannot be foretold with certainty in special cases, they are likely to be present in some form, and the most usual form (lacking positive side information to the contrary) is the kind of fixation model whereby responsiveness to such impacts declines with age. Since constraints of some sort must be placed on the cohort inference problem to render it tractable, constraints which recognize such a likelihood are undoubtedly more palatable than mathematical artifices which do not.

NOTES

1. Figure 4 is constructed as was Figure 1, according to the practices described in Appendix B. In this new figure, however, we have split up the Gallup samples more finely in the critical early period, and added other embellishments.

2. Although the early 1965 study bears all the hallmarks of a standard steady-state sample, where age and party identification strength are concerned, it is the sole sample of its type which did not figure in our earlier steady-state calculations, mainly because those calculations were completed some time before we became aware that the 1965 study had included the party identification item and hence added its results to our cohort file.

3. See Riley (1973: 44) for a discussion of the "compositional fallacy."

4. To protect against misinterpretation, I should emphasize the fact that we are addressing here no more than the *direct compositional effects* of the baby boom. A variety of hypotheses can be raised involving indirect effects (e.g., earlier changes in socialization about authority or the political system due to

boom-prompted changes in family structure or overloaded school systems, etc.), and of course our empirical demonstration is not at all tailored to the examination of such possibilities.

5. The subject is much more cumbersome to discuss than it might be but for the marked tendency of recent years, particularly under the rubric "adult socialization," to include as forms of "socialization" everything that a decade ago was called "attitude change," including the shifting opinions of the elderly about systems and processes with which they have had life-long familiarity and even participation. If "socialization" were instead restricted to its original meaning, which involved the anticipatory learnings, assumptions and feelings upon original introduction to a social system (a definition which, incidentally, allows for all manner of "adult socialization," as is witnessed by the sixty-year-old person elected for the first time to a legislative body, who must depend on a lot of learning of a purely introductory sort as to how the system operates, in order to participate effectively in it), then period effects as we have defined them would not automatically become "socialization" and hence the same class of event as the initial, anticipatory learnings of the six-year-old. With this current confusion in vogue, we must pile up verbiage to make what are entirely simple arguments.

6. We have not seen this effect directly as yet, but will below.

7. If in inspecting a trend line which implicitly allows twenty comparisons between neighboring points, and which is largely "smooth" save for one major anomaly, it is not much use to seize upon the anomaly and test it by standard statistical means to see if it is major enough to have occurred more than one time in twenty.

8. It should be mentioned for clarity's sake that no special form of smoothing has been employed with the raw data other than that which naturally arises from the combination of samples adjacent in time.

9. It should be emphasized that the initial measurement in the summer of 1965 shows ratings of Johnson's handling of Vietnam which lag notably behind ratings of Johnson's overall performance. With the latter indicator declining, and with ratings of Johnson's Vietnam policy remaining constant for a period, the two trends rapidly meet, and thereafter over the full course of Johnson's administration, they move in close tandem. A circumstantial argument could be built that had ratings of Johnson's Vietnam performance been monitored from six months earlier, they would have showed a sharp "leading" drop in the spring of 1965, temporarily distinguishing them from ratings of his overall performance although, presumably, acting to drag down the latter ratings as time progressed. This contention is not entirely fanciful, given the later performance of the two measures along with what happened in the spring of 1965. But I shall hew here to the available evidence.

10. I recognize that I have not addressed what appears in Figure 8 to be the first wave of the second shock prior to the 1972 election, centered among the young. Strictly speaking, this could also be Watergate, since the catalyzing burglary had already been discovered and its suspicious nature aired in the press. However, I do not find this interpretation compelling. For one thing, the public lies of President Nixon and his top aides had largely succeeded in covering up the true meaning of the burglary, at least until after the election. More important still,

the epicenter of this piece of the impact—among younger Democrats—does not fit in an obvious way with crimes conducted under apparent Republican Party auspices, or with the later clear Watergate responses. It is certain that some of what registers at this phase of the impact is the routine oscillation of the identification measure with the short-term political tides going into a landslide election, an effect which always registers more sharply with the young and with the disfavored party (in 1972. the Democrats). I remain unconvinced, however, that this accounts for all of the observed impact of this first phase.

Chapter 5

NOTES ON THE
PARTISAN DIRECTION COMPONENT

At the outset of this book I observed that party identification is a particularly charming workhorse for cohort
analysis because it is not one variable but two, since it
encapsulates a strength component and a direction component; and because these two components, when properly
analyzed with respect to cohort inference, yield contrasting
conclusions.[1] If the race is seen as one between routine
life-cycle changes on one hand, and imprints associated with
membership in birth cohorts on the other, as the older
literature construed the problem, then the direction component has over the period of observation been primarily a
cohort matter, while the strength component at least to 1965
has been primarily a life-cycle matter. The latter is true in
spite of a recent mainstream of conclusions to the contrary.

Since the prevalent recent errors in solution have involved
the strength component, I have spent most of our space

reviewing that element. We shall push through no comparably strenuous reanalyses of the direction component. By and large, this corner of inquiry has drifted back to what I see as the accurate conclusion concerning the relative dominance of birth cohort over life-cycle processes, after a period of some vagrancy.

However, certain discordant notes have been struck in the past few years, chiefly by Knoke and Hout (1974). We shall use this chapter first to clarify why the Knoke-Hout conclusions seem somewhat askew with respect to the general trend of other reported results concerning the direction component, and to argue that the main discordant conclusion emerging from their work is not to be taken very seriously. We shall then spend the remainder of the chapter sketching in some of the gambits that might be followed with the direction component once beyond the primal question of life-cycle vs. cohort effects.

Short-Term Oscillations in the Direction Component

The Knoke-Hout results are discordant in two particulars, one major and one minor. The minor discrepancy arises in the fact that these investigators, working within an analysis format which is best equipped of any currently available to disentangle age, period and cohort effects at the price of a few not-too-frightening assumptions, lay bare a faint life-cycle contribution to the static positive relationship between age and Republicanism. I see this as a minor revision, albeit a highly interesting one, since their data continue to show birth cohorts as contributing about twice as much to an accounting of total variance in the percent Democratic over the 1952-1972 period. Thus if the finding is taken without further examination, it does not contest the current wisdom that the cohort contribution is primary. Rather, it serves to dispute any contention that there is no life-cycle contribution whatever, a flatter assertion than most cohort analysts have dared to make.

The major discordant note, however, is that the Knoke-Hout partitioning shows that *neither* cohort *nor* life cycle contributes to the total variance being examined by anything like as much as do *period* effects. Indeed, period effects taken alone account for nearly as much variance as that attributable to both cohort and life-cycle effects summed together! This potentially represents a major revision of existing understandings of the proper cohort diagnosis for the direction component.

However, for those who have some familiarity with the dynamics of the party identification measure, the reasons for such a seemingly discrepant result lie very close to the surface. It is thoroughly dependent upon the joint effects of (a) a time-sampling problem; and (b) a failure to appreciate what is conceptually important variance in the direction component and what is not.

The Time-Sampling Problem. In the preceding chapter I had occasion to note that the central tendency of the party identification variable's direction component, as measured repeatedly over time, has a tendency to oscillate slightly in manifest tune with short-term variations in party fortunes, as independently indexed by national voting outcomes. The amplitude of this wobble is generally quite slight (within a percent or two), although it increases discernibly when measures are made close to any biennial national election, and is greater when the national election is the presidential one, rather than the off-year congressional election. Even when measurements are drawn close to presidential elections, however, the degree of wobble toward the favored party remains in an absolute sense quite slight, save in the case of landslide presidential elections, when the amplitude widens still further, reasonably enough. Hopefully it goes without saying that while the swings in the party identification measure are embarrassingly large in an absolute sense if one does not understand their sources, relative to the corresponding swings in the national vote division they still remain very small.[2]

As was also noted in the preceding chapter, the short-term swings in the direction component associated with the landslide elections of 1956, 1968 and 1972 have been momentarily large enough to have some clear definition in spite of sampling error, and they have shown certain regularities. In all three cases, a swing in the direction of the ultimate landslide-winning party of a magnitude which exceeds any others in the record, was already visible in spring samples preceding the actual presidential election involved, which is to say before the identity of competing candidates had become certain. Thus, with three successful predictions out of three, the wobble has tentative interest as a lead indicator. In all three cases the swing visible in the spring was maintained (but not increased) as of the standard pre-election survey in the weeks before the day of the landslide. We have less regular samples available just after these elections. In one case (1964) a survey carried out seven to eleven weeks after the landslide still showed the fall swing nearly, if not completely intact. In this instance, nearly two years elapse before the next survey, by which time all of the swing has evaporated, and mean party identification is back within a percentage point of its grand mean for the entire period. In the other two cases, when the first post-election surveys occurred six to eleven months after the landslide election, all signs of the swing had already vanished.

Thus these swings are both very marked and very fleeting. Other oscillations do occur, typically associated with other presidential elections, far less marked but equally transient. Outside of the immediate context of national elections, the mean of the direction component in each new reading moves within an impressively narrow range around the central tendency of such individual means for the intermediate period involved.

We have been aware of these oscillations for about twenty years, since the first major one was observable in 1956. As we shall see shortly, we know enough about them that for most

although not all purposes they can be taken as no more than
a measurement annoyance. Indeed, for virtually all long-term,
cross-time assessments of the sort that interest cohort
analysts, it is wisest to adjust away these wobbles from the
data at the outset.

The time sample represented by the studies used by Knoke
and Hout for their computations could scarcely be better
calculated to provide an enormously biassed magnification of
these wobbles. Not only were all of the six studies employed
carried out in the most immediate time proximity to national
elections; they were even limited to the presidential elections
of the twenty-year period. Three of the six were landslides.

The impact this time bias has upon the Knoke-Hout results
is easy to demonstrate. If we look at the cross-time variance
in aggregate percentage Democratic among party identifiers over all of the studies in my large cohort file
for the same 1952-1972 period involved in the Knoke-Hout
work, and compare this with the same variance in the subset
of six presidential election studies used by these investigators,
we find that the variance in the subset of six is nearly half
again as large as in the total series. Even this is not a very
incisive comparison, since for institutional reasons my total
cohort file is itself enormously biassed toward proximity to
national presidential elections, relative to a hypothetical
random time sample of observation points in the period, or
any set of studies generated by monitoring at regular and
frequent intervals. In all, barely one-half of these studies in
my file were carried out at least ten months before a
presidential election, or at least three months thereafter.
However, if we calculate the aggregate-level variance in
percent Democratic of party identifications for this subset
sheltered from the presidential-election wobbles and compare
it again with the six presidential election studies, we find that
such a variance in the studies used by Knoke and Hout is
nearly five times as large! In any system of, say, monthly
monitorings, less than 30 percent of the observation times

would fall even within the wide band of time from ten months before a presidential election to three months afterward. For the Knoke-Hout time "sample," 100 percent of the observations lie within some few weeks of a presidential election.

The exaggeration of the total variance tied up in short-term wobbles in the Knoke-Hout estimations is necessarily enormous; yet it is these wobbles that their analytic technique discriminates as short-term "period effects" in the direction component of party identification. Thus it is not surprising that their summary results are quite heterodox in the importance attributed to these period effects, relative to life-cycle or birth-cohort contributions.

The Conceptual Status of Short-Term Oscillations. Even if Knoke and Hout had worked with raw materials that put the presidential oscillations of the direction component in a more proper time perspective, they would have continued to represent at least some small fraction of the total variance. Yet there is further serious question whether conceptually this portion of the variance is even relevant in a substantive sense.

Obviously, these wobbles are a "real" part of the historical record, and it requires a rather strong argument to defend the possibility that they might well be expunged from the record before analysis is even begun. I shall not make an all-purpose argument in this direction. Indeed, I have already pointed out that as distant early warnings of presidential landslides, these wobbles may be almost priceless in their empirical value. But most cohort analysts of long-term data on party identification are not engaged in short-term predictions of specific election outcomes. Instead, they are interested in the long-term evolution of the partisan coloration of the voting population in the country. And it is in these terms that the observed oscillations in the direction component are next to irrelevant.

We have already seen that these swings toward the

momentarily-favored party—even the large landslide ones—
seem to disappear almost completely from reports of party
identification within a few months of the election excitation.
This fact alone raises severe doubts as to the utility of data
contaminated by any such particular swing for even intermediate prediction, much less long-term estimations. But the
clinching point emerges when we take more detailed note as
to how the more marked of these oscillations tend to arise at
all.

It has long been clear that there is a small but significant
fraction—probably over 10 percent, but under 25 percent—of
the American population which is so remote from psychological participation in national political life that the notion
of an abiding loyalty to a political party which underlies the
party identification measure is next to meaningless. When
posed the party identification question in an interview
situation, many of this remnant give responses which
properly get them coded as "apolitical" or, as is a bit more
misleading, as "independents." Others, however, play along
by picking a party, and the party picked is very likely to be
the party which they perceive as riding high at the moment.
Of course, these people are so inattentive to national political
life that they bring almost no information whatever to the
question as to which party is for the moment "riding high."
The only cues are the most gross and simplistic ones, such as
which party occupies the White House at the moment. And
even this gross information lacks much saliency for these
people, save in the heat of an oncoming election, when this
information is daily news fare. The party identification
question posed to these people does not evoke a report of
abiding loyalty to one of the parties, but rather at best a
statement as to how they would vote, were they required to
vote at the moment. And in the main, they would vote with
the incumbent president, whichever party he may represent,
unless he is under some enormous stench of which they
happen to be aware. The capping irony to this syndrome is,

of course, that these are people who never have and never will actually cast a vote, even for president.

I do not intend to argue that but for chronic nonvoters, no oscillations whatever in the direction component of party identification would be observed. But I am quite prepared to argue that a small remnant of such chronic nonvoters is responsible—not completely, but by a vast disproportion—for the fact that the amplitude of the oscillations in the direction component are as large as they are in an absolute sense (if relatively, they remain quite small).

The evidence for such a contention is, as it seems to me, simply massive. Since all of it has been published at least once before, and frequently more than once, I shall try to be both brief and selective.

Let us consider two types of facts. In the Roosevelt-Truman era, Democratic party strategists were frustrated by the poll-developed knowledge that nonvoters were by rather massive margins Democratic in their preferences. It seemed that if only this reservoir of votes could be tapped, many narrow losses could be turned into victories. In the first Eisenhower-Stevenson contest in 1952, with the Republicans winning handily, nonvoter preferences for president remained slightly Democratic (52-48). The perception of sure Democratic votes in the nonvoter ranks was pricked decisively, however, when in 1956 the nonvoters shifted to a 72-28 split favoring the Republicans. While 1956 was a landslide victory for the Republicans even in the actual vote, the magnitude of the movement among nonvoters between the two years absolutely dwarfed the change in the actual vote. It is clear that the nonvoting segment of the population is quite unanchored, and capable of vast changes in partisan preference in response to short-term political tides although, as in the 1952-1956 sequence, this response tends to be visibly lagged relative to the rest of the electorate, presumably because the information as to which party is "riding high" permeates only more slowly to those psychologically remote from the process.

The other set of facts involves the party identification measure itself and its individual-level stability over time, as we have been able to measure it by a national panel sample between 1956 and 1960. Perhaps the best way to sort out a set of chronic nonvoters from such a sample is to isolate the set of persons old enough to have been eligible for several national presidential elections, yet who confess that they have never voted in any one of them. While the probability that some future vote may be cast by some members of such a subset is obviously not zero, there is evidence that such a probability is extremely low. Within the set of people thirty and over who report having voted for president at least "frequently," the individual-level continuity correlation *(r)* in party identification reports over a four-year span falls in the upper .80's. While this does not represent perfect stability, it does not leave much room for a high incidence of shifts several steps across the party identification scale, and hence little room for a contribution to short-term oscillations in the balance between the two parties. Among those thirty and over who have only but "seldom" voted in presidential elections, this correlation falls to .76. Among those who have never voted for president despite at least two or three options to do so, the correlation is .36, a value which leaves much room for a fair incidence of large leaps across the scale of the sort which can indeed create notable swings in the marginals of party identification, to the degree that such large leaps tend to be unidirectional in response to immediate political tides.

The conceptual problem, therefore, is obvious. Readers of cohort analyses concerning the partisanship of the American electorate naturally presume they are learning something about voting behavior and the electorate. Hence the high-lighting of findings that are largely attributable to persons who by self-selection never take part in the active electorate or engage in any "voting behavior" whatever seems rather misleading. It is in this context, and for these reasons, that we largely ignore these short-term oscillations, and often feel justified in adjusting them out of long-term calculations.

It is for these reasons as well that the main discordant result in the Knoke-Hout findings, although perfectly intelligible in terms of the raw materials used, need not command serious attention. With a more representative sample of time points, there is every reason to believe that the relatively large amount of variance tied up in these short-term oscillations in their data base would shrink very substantially. And of that variance which would remain from this shrinkage, only a small further fraction would be of conceptual interest in any event, since much of it would be arising from people not in the active electorate or indulging in voting behavior. It is hard to know exactly what a joint correction of the time sampling problem and an initial elimination from the data of chronic nonvoters would actually do in a repeat of the Knoke-Hout calculations, since our hasty diagnostic calculations in this chapter involve changes in aggregate-level variances, while their more detailed estimations properly involve partitionings of individual-level variance. I strongly doubt that their period-effect contribution would entirely disappear; indeed, I would be dismayed if it did. But I would suspect with equal strength that such recalculation would leave their period-effect contribution no longer the strongest of the three by an impressive margin; rather, it would sink below the cohort or pure-generation contribution, and probably below the age or life-cycle contribution as well. In any event, the change would almost certainly come to square their results with other post-Crittenden conclusions that the dominant effect on the direction component is of the classic generational sort.

True Period Effects and the Direction Component

While much of the variance in short-term oscillations of the direction component is contributed by people who never vote, and hence has a peculiar conceptual status, the historical record of these oscillations does have further interest for the cohort analyst of the active electorate. Indeed, it is ironic that swings in preference among those who never vote is such a sensitive barometer, albeit often quite lagged, of the short-term forces which register as one-sided defections among voting identifiers or as shifts in preference among independents. Thus the nonvoter swings have their counterpart, although somewhat muffled, in swings of the actual vote. And these short-term changes in relative party fortunes, as they bear on the active electorate, are in fact candidates as classic "period effects" on the direction component of party identification.

It has long been recognized, and endlessly documented both here and abroad, that responsiveness to these short-term swings in party fortunes among those who actually vote tends to be greater for the young than for the old. In fact, it is useful heuristically to think of the adult population in three broad segments: chronic nonvoters of all ages, who are least anchored in the party system and who are capable of the most dramatic responses to short-term tides (although often rather tardily); young voters who are only weakly anchored through family political traditions and but brief experience, whose responsiveness is less dramatic yet abundantly clear; and older voters whose responsiveness is least.

Of course this description merely recapitulates, in another vocabulary, the earlier discussions of life-cycle changes in the strength component, since a strong identification is an anchor against responsiveness to short-term change. And it argues strongly that the direction component of party identification, under the impacts of immediate "period effects" favoring one party or the other, shows the same declining responsiveness to change with age with characterizes the Carlsson-Karlsson (1970) "fixation model." Indeed, one of the main exhibits those investigators use to defend the plausibility of such a model involves voting swings among young and old, and hence a partisan direction component.

Once again we arrive at a juncture where the blur between period and generation effects becomes painful. For if period impacts are strongest upon new entrants to the voting system, and if these impacts have any permanency, then of course today's generation effects are nothing more than yesterday's period effects. It is in this light that the short-term oscillations in party fortunes, as indexed dramatically by nonvoters, or less dramatically by swings in the actual vote, have potential for longer-range significance. In the ideal case, it would seem at least possible that a complete history of two generations of short-term swings in party fortunes might be "archeologically" reconstructed by a finely-enough partitioned cohort analysis of a sufficiently large sample drawn at any single point in time.

In our cohort analyses for *The American Voter* we had pyramided all available samples (1952-1958) organized by birth cohort, and looked at the behavior of the direction component (proportion of three strengths of Democratic identifiers to the total of identifiers) by annual cohort. For nearly a thirty-year period we had about 200 cases for each birth year, and with very little further smoothing[3] the results were quite dramatic. For the oldest cohorts, born near or before the turn of the century, the graph showed a low (relatively Republican) plateau, with only minor hills and valleys. For the younger cohorts there was a high (relatively Democratic) plateau, again with minor hills and valleys. These two relatively flat plateaus were joined in the middle by a very steep cliff, handsomely localized in these data among those born between the years 1905 and 1912. Needless to say, these cohorts were obviously the newest entrants to the voting system at the time of the Great Depression and its fabled attendant partisan realignment.

The sharpness of definition of this "cliff" meant that it was relatively easy, even with only a span of six years of observations, to determine that the cliff was increasing in chronological age while remaining constantly located with respect to birth year, rather than the reverse. And it was this assessment which produced the judgment that the principal determinant of the static relationship between age and the direction component at the time was generational, rather than life cycle.

The steepness of the "cliff" between the 1905 and 1912 cohorts naturally invited other analyses which we did not have space to publish at the time. If the 1932 realignment registered in such a remarkably localized fashion for the new entrants of the period even when evaluated twenty to twenty-five years later, the question immediately arose as to whether the minor hills and valleys along the low early plateau or the high later plateau were not also dimmer reflections of other historical shifts in party fortunes. They did not involve great year-to-year variation, and technically could be seen as within the range of sampling error. Nevertheless, there was a late downturn among those born after 1930 that could be seen as reflecting the new entrants to the Eisenhower period, and other minor downturns in the earliest part of the record that could be loosely imagined as reflecting familiar pre-1920 Republican swings.

Therefore we prepared a synthetic amalgam of presidential and congressional election results back into the nineteenth century, designed to capture as best we could the short-term swings in party tides on a biennial basis over the whole period. One of the chief enjoyments in fitting this voting curve to the direction component curve (and the optimal fit was substantial: an r exceeding .5) was to see at what number of years lag between birth and voting outcomes the fit was empirically maximized. In large part because of the sharpness of the "cliff" in the party identification data on one hand, and the Democratic nadir of the mid-1920s rising to high-water marks in the early 1930s in the voting record on the other, the point of fit between the two curves was itself very sharply localized (cf. Figure 11). It lay between a lag of twenty-one and twenty-two years, a result which was of

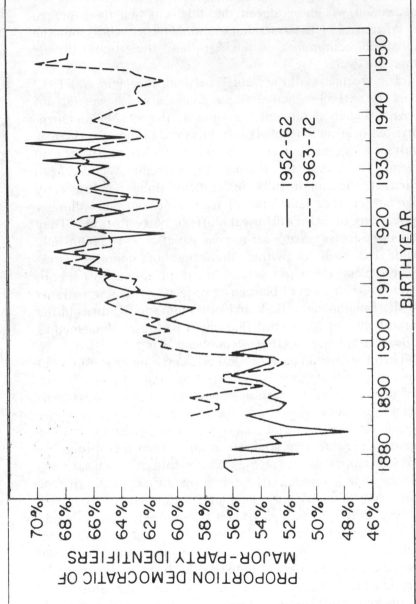

Figure 10: PARTISANSHIP BY BIRTH COHORT, IN RECENT AND EARLIER DATA BATCHES

course intuitively superb, as it fell at the exact statutory age of entry to the voting system which pertained at the time.

Apart from the Crittenden interlude, most cohort analysts of the direction component have had little trouble finding this distinctive Depression Generation and confirming its birth-cohort base. However, virtually all analyses I have seen deal with relatively gross birth cohorts (four, five or even ten years "wide"), and these treatments tend to blur away the original beauty of the sharp localization of these Depression effects. Therefore, it has seemed worthwhile, by way of terminating this brief discussion of the direction component, to report on updatings of these analyses with the benefit of nearly twenty years additional cohort data.

Perhaps the most important single message to be derived from these further analyses is that the sharpness of definition of the Depression-related "cliff" has been progressively deteriorating over the past two decades. This message is documented in Figure 10, where we have divided our cohort data from the 1952-1972 period into roughly equal halves, according to whether they were collected before or after 1963. Even the first curve shows a less focussed cliff than we originally observed in the 1952-1958 segment of the data, since it includes a number of later studies up through 1962. If the 1952-1958 segment suggested a localization of effects between 1905 and 1912, the larger 1952-1962 segment only suggests a vaguer localization from about 1901 to 1916. The segment of data collected over the second decade after 1952, while it still clearly shows that something major happened among new Depression entrants, is fuzzier still, with a transition from one plateau to the other now merely appearing to have occurred sometime between the birth years from 1897 to 1915.

Given the decade of erosion in the clarity of the Depression transition, what happens when we replicate the fitting of our synthetic vote trend to the birth-cohort trend in the direction component of party identification using data

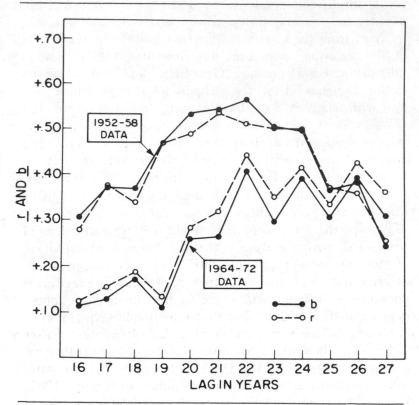

Figure 11: FINDING THE OPTIMAL LAG BETWEEN BIRTH YEAR AND
PARTISAN CHANGES IN THE NATIONAL VOTE, WITH
RECENT AND EARLIER DATA BATCHES

from the later period rather than the earlier follows in the
most obvious way. In Figure 11 we graph our original data
computed nearly twenty years ago with the birth-cohort
trend as it originally appeared over the span of observations
from 1952 through 1958 (*not*, as in Figure 10, the full
segment of data 1952-1962). Here the localization of optimal
fit was extremely clear at the point of displacement of the
two series by twenty-one or twenty-two years: any displacement of the two series by two years more or less than these
figures produced a very marked decline in the goodness of fit.

Figure 11 also shows the same optimizing operation conducted on data solely drawn from studies conducted in the 1964-1972 period, or the later trend line in Figure 10. Here, if one had to pick a single lag between the two series which produces an optimal fit, the lag would still be gauged as one of twenty-two years, essentially the same as before. However, the overall goodness of fit at the optimal point has deteriorated markedly, and one could choose a lag of anywhere from twenty-two years to twenty-six years without much loss in the fit.[4] All of this follows in a direct way from the less clearly defined transition in the later data, along with the asymmetric blurring toward the older side (birth years 1897 to 1905, or people in their later twenties or early thirties at the time of the Depression) of the transition.

The fact that the original sharp localization of the transition as it was observed in the mid-1950s has been blurring progressively within more recent data collections is not in itself surprising. In fact, several quite plausible but independent mechanisms would tend to erode the contours of such a transition as it became increasingly remote in time, and I can think of no plausible mechanisms which could be expected to compensate for such erosion by progressively sharpening the definition as it faded in time.

One such eroding mechanism is tied up with the accuracy of reporting of personal age. The studies in our cohort file have elicited birth year in various ways. In some, the birth year is directly elicited. In others, age is requested, and then birth year is deduced from it. In either case, but particularly the second, there is some minor margin for error in deducing the actual age of the respondent as of November election time, especially for studies conducted in the springtime. More important still, it is almost certain that the precision of age reports declines progressively as respondents become older, and an increasing rate of misassignments of birth years by wider and wider margins among the older respondents would necessarily blur the clarity of any birth-year contours.

Quite apart from the report accuracy problem, one of the clear derivations from the Carlsson-Karlsson fixation model is that adjacent cohorts which may have been quite distinct from one another in their earlier years on some attribute, will tend to converge increasingly as they age, producing a "blurring of cohort identity" also mentioned by Ryder (1965). Again, our observed data are nicely compatible with such a prediction.

I have in fact experimented briefly with the Carlsson-Karlsson model, using as input "stimulus pressures" over time derived from the synthetic voting series designed to replicate the ebb and flow of party fortunes, along with the age-dependent change-proneness parameters used by those investigators. Of course the latter vector of values was intended to be no more than illustrative, and any number of gradients declining with age would be generally compatible with the fixation principle. But it may be worth reporting that the amount of decay in the Depression transition over the relevant decade between the 1950s and 1960s shown by the model run with the published illustrative values does not begin to match the amount of blurring actually observed in Figure 10. To provide a better fit, a substantial amount of change-proneness would have to endure farther into middle age. Even then, the asymmetry of the decay (greater erosion to the older side of the transition) is not predicted by the model, although it is likely that further attention to accuracy of age reporting could help to improve the prediction. In general, it would be of interest to attempt to estimate fixation parameters that would correspond to the observed decay.[5]

We may also profitably examine segments of the birth-year cohort function apart from the clear Depression transition, to see whether other shifts in party fortunes before or since have left any characteristic imprints. A glance at Figure 10 is not particularly encouraging in this regard.[6] Variations along the pre-Depression plateau (birth year before 1900) are hard to evaluate because of declining case numbers. For the plateau running from 1917 to 1937 there are ample cases in both series of observations of Figure 10 (200-300 cases per birth year) to provide reasonable stability. Yet the (r) between the two series is −.01, or no relationship whatever, despite the fact that the voting record at the time the relevant respondents were young and malleable was showing rather marked fluctuations or short-term period effects in preferences. Thus if the fine-grain variations in the direction component along this plateau involve anything more than pure sampling error, the deflections are too fleeting to survive a ten-year gap in observations. Apparently it is rare that short-term period impacts on the direction component leave a permanent trace in the cohort record which can later be interpreted as "generational."

Of course this negative result may be taken to enhance our appreciation of the enormous impact of the Depression on American partisanship. Such a contrast in the durability of an imprint is not particularly surprising, given the long recognition of the period around 1932 as that of profound realignment, unlike most of the swings of the popular vote before or since.

In this regard, there is another intriguing peculiarity in the birth-year record of the direction component not visible in Figure 10. If one combines all data in the file (instead of splitting it into two halves, as in Figure 10) and pushes the examination backward to those born before 1880, one major new anomaly emerges. This is an enormous dip or pro-Republican bias centering particularly in 1875 and 1876. Case numbers here are few, and perhaps the dip should be totally ignored. Nonetheless, there are for example twenty-nine independent cases of party identifiers born in 1875, and only 24 percent of them are Democratic. In 1876, the figure is 39 percent, still well below the plateau characteristic of the pre-1900 birth-year period. We mention this dip for a simple reason. If political scientists were asked what realignment next preceded the 1932 political cataclysm, the normal verdict would be the election of 1896, which favored the Republicans. And of course the persons born in 1875 and 1876 were twenty and twenty-one years of age in 1896.

This may be utter coincidence. After all, while the Depression transition is still extremely visible, we have seen that its once-sharp contours have eroded considerably a mere quarter-century after the critical events had transpired. Surely if we add another quarter-century of erosion time, as we must for the 1896 case, we might not expect to find much of a tell-tale imprint left. Yet the timing of this dip is uncanny, if it is merely due to a sampling bounce associated with very limited case numbers. And we could grant the conceivability of a good 15 percent underestimate of the proportion Democratic, due to sampling error for these cohorts, and still have a deviation in the record which would rival in momentary magnitude that found for the more amply documented Depression transition. It is a pity that the appropriate measurements of party identification on good samples were not drawn a decade or two sooner, for then a more solid assessment of the long-term generational impact of a second realignment would be available.

Conclusions

If all shifts in relative party fortunes, registering in the national vote as short-term effects, left a lasting imprint on at least the newest entrants to the voting system as of the time of impact, then we could arrive at intriguing computations as to what it would profit a given party to nominate some particularly charismatic candidate, or achieve some other noteworthy triumph, in terms of vote increments ten, twenty and thirty years later.

However, the evidence reviewed in this chapter suggests that almost all such short-term period effects disappear from the record with the speed of castles in the sand. It is only at the rare moments of realignment that a more permanent imprint is laid down. Among other implications, one is that if no new major realignment intrudes within the next decade, the static correlation between age and the direction component of party identification, so long a staple feature of the American political scene, will very nearly, if not completely, wither away.

NOTES

1. As one result of their thorough analysis, Knoke and Hout (1974: 710) are led to the conclusion that "the processes pushing the population toward a non-party identification differ from those leading to a choice among Democrats, Republicans and Independents."

2. Knoke and Hout (1974), impressed by the amplitude of these swings in their data, seem surprised that according to *The American Voter,* "party identifications were less subject to short-term changes than were voting preferences" (p. 706). While we shall momentarily show that the kind of raw comparisons between vote change and party identification change that the authors have in mind are largely irrelevant, the fact remains that the 1952-1972 variance in the two-party division of the national vote, laid against the parallel variance in the party identification maximized by looking at it only for the same election periods, is still nearly six times as great. This contrast would seem ample to support the generalization that voting preferences are more unstable than party identification.

3. Although the raw data came from annual birth cohorts, we settled the curve down a bit by a three-year moving average transformation. For comparative purposes, we use the same convention in Figure 10 to follow.

4. The reader should not be too put off by the sawtooth effect which arises in the later stages of the fitting exploration for the 1964-1972 data in Figure 11. The synthetic vote series yields observations only at biennial intervals, whereas the birth-cohort series on the direction component has observations for each birth year. As the degree of lag is varied from an odd number of years to an even number and back again, *there is an alternation in the birth-cohort series being used.* Figure 11 merely indicates that where the 1964-1972 comparisons are concerned, the odd-numbered birth years included some more sharply-discrepant or poorly-fitting data points than the even-numbered birth years.

5. The specific Carlsson-Karlsson model structure is only one of several possibilities compatible with the fixation principle, and not necessarily the best. Among detailed peculiarities of that model is a tendency to accord the most recent stimulus an implicit weight which, by middle age, begins to move toward an order of magnitude greater than the next-most-recent stimulus. Such an

implicit assumption has no obvious psychological counterpart and induces at least a faint level of odd counter-motions under some stimulus sequences. A more palatable model might deal with a descending sequence of weights for each new experience. Such a model would initially behave much as the Carlsson-Karlsson model, but would subsequently show some divergences.

6. The reader might well keep in mind in examining Figure 10, that both curves are more ragged near their beginning and end simply because case numbers are declining near these extremes. For the purposes of that figure, we have used a minimum of 100 independent cases per birth year as a cutting-point for beginning and ending the series.

Chapter 6

SOME CONCLUSIONS

I shall refrain from any thorough recapitulation of major points made during the course of this book. However, there are a few broad implications arising from the ground covered that deserve to be gathered up by way of conclusion. Consistent with the dual focus of this book, some of these implications are substantive, involving the political ramifications of observed changes in party identification. Others are methodological, involving the strategy and tactics of cohort analysis. Let us briefly consider both, in the order given.

Selected Political Implications

Some cohort analysts explicitly eschew the stating of broader implications in party identification change. In other cases, a different form of uncertainty is manifested. Thus, for example, Knoke and Hout (1974: 710) express dismay at the small proportion of the total variance in partisan preferences accounted for even when life-cycle, period and generation effects are laid end to end, although they do affirm a faith that the results are not totally unimportant.

I think that faith is well-placed, and the reasons for my judgment are simple. It is true that the Knoke-Hout estimates of these "demographic" contributions are in one sense minimized, since any overlap between these demographic contributions and a set of seven rather strong sociostructural predictors is assigned by the investigators to the latter. Thus the small demographic contributions are what remains net of any overlapping effects. Any revision of this fairly arbitrary assumption would only increase the apparent variance controlled by the demographic or cohort factors. I do not think, however, that the increase would be very startling even if this decision were totally reversed. And I would be content to argue that nonetheless, such a small portion of variance controlled is more than substantively trivial.

This is true for two reasons. One is that such demographic or cohort factors provide firmer leverage for the prediction of change than any of the sociostructural factors. Where the sociostructural factors are concerned, the safest prediction is usually one of "no change," as the Knoke-Hout results show, except in those instances where demographic considerations —the relative expansion or dying out of politically distinctive population groups—intrude to suggest change. And whereas marked change in the partisan coloration of some subgroups in the society does occur from time to time, foreseeing such change before it begins is next to impossible. However, many features of the processes of "demographic metabolism" are inexorable, and often can yield up compelling predictions of change for at least the intermediate term.

The second reason why even small amounts of variance tied up with such demographic processes can be substantively important is because of the nature of political competition itself. One of the chief motives—although not the only one—for a substantive interest in party identification is of course to illuminate the outcomes of party competition, such as which party is likely to control the Congress or occupy the White House. For such an interest, the action is almost completely at the margins, and frequently involves very small percentage differences in the vote division around the magic 50-50 mark. In two of the last four presidential elections, for example, the winner of the two-party vote division exceeded that magic mark by less than one-half of one percent. Presumably if the basic partisan coloration of the active electorate had differed by as much as one percent one way or the other in these elections, the whole system would have proceeded down the opposite partisan fork from the path actually taken. Hence even minuscule shifts in the partisanship of the electorate can have major political ramifications; and to the degree that such tiny shifts can be deduced in advance from links to demographic processes, even these faint links can be of great substantive importance.

In general, the broad political implications of small percentage shifts in the partisan coloration of the active electorate—as indexed by the party division in the direction component—are easier to grasp intuitively than are the implications of the recent changes in the strength component of party identification. While implications of change in both components could be spelled out in a great variety of directions, we shall limit ourselves here to one cluster of political implications that is very central, at least in the sense of playing upon change in the two components either jointly or interdependently.

The conceptual machinery that we will require for this exercise is quite simple. Let us suppose that we would like to compute in advance the ceteris paribus odds of either the Republicans or Democrats winning in the two-party popular vote division in any given national election. The first thing we would want to know, of course, is which party is the favorite of a majority of the electorate, since it is unlikely that underlying partisanship stands balanced exactly at 50-50. However, if we are going to engage in a computation of more precise odds, as opposed to observing crudely that one party has a better chance than the other because it is known to be majoritarian, then we would of course have an intense interest in the more exact magnitude of that majority. That is, other things equal, a party with an underlying majority of 51-49, while undoubtedly to be favored, obviously has less strong chances of winning any single election than a party with a 55-45 underlying majority edge. The direction component of party identification, properly treated to set aside useless partisan advantage among chronic nonvoters, is a direct indicator of the magnitude of the underlying "effective" majority.

But this parameter of the system is not all we would need to know. To compute precise odds, we would also want to know how much play around the central tendency of the vote division is typically touched off by responses of the voters to short-term shifts in party fortunes. If the electorate is extremely unresponsive to such shifts, then even a tiny majority of 51-49 might suffice to give the majority party 90-10 odds of winning any given election, other things equal. If the electorate is extremely responsive, however, then even a wide 55-45 majority might not be enough to place its odds of winning a given election as high as 60-40. In short, we need to have an expected variance for a large number of hypothetical election trials, as well as a central tendency. It is clear that such an expected variance is some inverse function of the strength component of party identification.

It is also true that the expected variance is in some measure a function of the type of election involved. It is well-recognized, for example, that the expected variance of the national vote division summed for congressional races is signficantly lower than that of the national vote division for president. This difference is the joint result of a number of

factors, all of which tend in the same direction. As often as
not (in off-year elections), congressional candidates are
responded to by a restricted electorate of higher than average
partisanship. Congressional candidates are on balance less
visible than presidential candidates, and hence less likely to
provoke defections across party lines. And finally, it matters
that a national division of the congressional vote is an aggregation over several hundred mini-elections, each affected in some
degree by local short-term forces, which in the aggregation
process tend to balance out in some degree, moving the
national outcome closer to the central tendency of the
partisan division.

With this conceptual machinery in hand, we can now
review the implications of the major cohort influences on the
two components of party identification since 1952. The
Democrats were already the clear majority party as of 1952,
enjoying a majority which is best estimated as having been
slightly over 53-47, where the active electorate was concerned. The main demographic pressure on this margin was
upward for the Democrats, because an aging Republican
generation was dying out, while incoming cohorts were by
comparison relatively Democratic. It is, of course, easy to
exaggerate the impact of this turnover, for as Knoke and
Hout imply, the age differences in the partisan component,
while unquestionably present, are not huge (on the order of
12 percent, as Figure 10 would indicate). It is scarcely as
though elderly people who are 100 percent Republican are
leaving the electorate to newcomers who are 100 percent
Democratic.

Nevertheless, this demographic interchange has favored the
Democrats. The effects are gentle enough in any intermediate
term to be quite obscured by the short-term oscillations in
the direction component discussed in the preceding chapter.
Still, there has been a basic upward trend in the proportion
Democratic which has averaged slightly over 0.1 percent per
annum since 1952, bringing the Democratic margin up
toward 56-44 by 1975.

While this shift approaching three percent may from some points of view seem terribly small, it is easy to understate its significance. Some of the significance should be apparent from our earlier mention of very narrow popular vote margins in some presidential elections. But it is also true that the zone through which the partisan component has been passing since 1952 is a peculiarly critical one. If it is appropriate to assume that the underlying population of hypothetical election outcomes is normally distributed about its current central tendency with a variance characteristic of the aggregate levels of party identification pertaining during the steady-state period, then the magic 50-50 mark has in the 1952-1975 period moved from a position less than one standard deviation from the central tendency, to a position greater than one standard deviation, where congressional voting is concerned. And for presidential voting, it has been coming up toward one standard deviation in the later stages of the shift.

The marker of one standard deviation is in turn peculiarly critical, because it is in this zone that the odds of the majority party winning are shifting most rapidly. If we stick for purposes of argument to the congressional variances relevant to the steady-state levels of partisan strength, then a change in the underlying Democratic majority from 53 percent to 56 percent reduces the Republican chances of capturing any given national congressional vote division faster than a superficially comparable shift from 50 percent to 53 percent, or from 56 percent to 59 percent, all because of the nonlinear shape of the normal curve, and its point of most rapid change around one standard deviation from the mean.

Thus on the face of it, the gradual upward trend in the Democratic majority in the third quarter of the century would seem to have moved the Democratic Party from a good position to a downright commanding one. However, at least two observations must yet be made, lest hasty conclusions be drawn.

One codicil important in its own right is that as of the time
of writing, this upward demographic pressure on the Democratic advantage has just about run its course. To be sure,
distinctively Republican elderly people remain in the electorate as of 1976, and will continue to disappear rapidly in
the future. However, if our data and diagnoses of generation
effects on the direction component of party identification
are correct (cf. Figure 10), the time in which the most
relatively Republican cohorts (or, perhaps, the least distinctively Democratic ones) are disappearing from the electorate
in the largest absolute numbers is already several years past.
The most distinctive cohorts that remain are already such
tiny remnants as of 1976 that their further attrition will have
negligible impact on the overall partisan coloration of the
population. There are larger fractions of the population
which are discriminably more Republican than the national
average, and which are just approaching the time of most
rapid disappearance. But they are much less distinctively
Republican than their immediate elders, so that their
disappearance will have more limited further effects. Thus,
while the demographic pressure favoring the Democrats has
not disappeared completely, and will not for some years, the
potency of this pressure is well past its highwater mark.

The second observation is considerably the more important, however. Our calculations of rates of change in the odds
of a Democratic victory in any given election were based on
the variances which pertained during the steady-state period.
However, that period also terminated, according to our
analyses, a decade ago, and the progressive weakening of
aggregate levels of the strength component mean that the
implicit variances governing such odds have been progressively increasing, thereby serving to move the odds associated
with any given degree of majority back toward the 50-50
mark.

I have not gone through the full calculations of these
changing odds, although more precise calculations of a

plausible sort can be made. However, it is far from evident that the odds of the Democrats capitalizing upon their majority in any given election are significantly better in 1975 or 1976 than they were at the beginning of the period, despite a near doubling of the size of their majority in the interim, and a very considerable gain in those odds which would have been implied but for the downturn in party loyalties begun in 1965. And still more to the point, our analyses toward the end of Chapter 4 imply that while the upward demographic pressures on the Democratic majority are dwindling toward a halt, for parallel demographic reasons the pressures toward continued declines in the aggregate strength of party loyalties are likely to remain strong. Hence whatever the Democratic odds of victory in any given election in the current period may be, they are certain to deteriorate further in the near future, short of unforeseeable new events that might either increase their majority or reverse the tide of declining party loyalties.

These are some of the major political implications of our analyses. As noted earlier, they could be spelled out in other directions as well. Thus, the decline in party loyalties has a variety of ramifications ranging from further increases in ticket-splitting and heightened incidence of legislatures and executives of opposing parties, all the way to sharpened anxieties among campaign strategists in the face of advancing levels of uncertainty. But the most central implications of the changing parameters of the two components of party identification have been made clear.

Implications for Cohort Analysis

This book was originally motivated by distress at the babel of contradictory verdicts that have arisen about the cross-time properties of party identification in the period since our first cohort analyses of that attribute for *The American Voter*. Such a babel is not uncommon in scientific inquiry where investigators are looking at quite different slicings of reality drawn from independently-conducted experimentation on the same general subject matter. But it is perhaps most painful where investigators are looking at the same body of data or, at the outside (as with the Gallup partisanship series), a closely related series.

Over the course of the book I naturally have been intent upon laying out my own view as to the most plausible cohort inferences concerning the party identification series. At the same time, it has seemed dreadfully important to address head-on the conflicts in testimony that have arisen from the same body of evidence. Indeed, that is where most of our space has gone. It would be unsettling if conflicts in testimony had been traced to major discrepancies in the root data. However, I cannot recall any instance in which this has been true. In each case of major discordance in conclusion, I have had no trouble, after reexamining my own large file, in seeing what it was the investigator involved was looking at, or failing to look at, in forming his conclusions. And from this portfolio of conflicting perceptions, we have put together a collation of the common woes of cohort inference.

It would be tempting to conclude that the babel of conflicting verdicts has arisen because of the fundamental indeterminacy of cohort inference itself: I suppose there is a minor grain of truth in such an observation, but I would have trouble defending it very strenuously, for it seems to me that most of the problems we have catalogued are of a more elemental sort. If this paper had achieved some miraculous demonstration that the party identification series would only be rendered intelligible by some diabolical congeries of interactions between life-cycle, period and birth-cohort influences, then it would indeed be proper to argue that past confusions have arisen because of a failure to recognize how complex—and indeterminate—the inference problem was.

Quite to the contrary, however, this book has argued in the main that the observed data are handsomely compatible with models involving relatively simple effects, with the possible exception of the post-1965 performance of the strength component, and that to a reasonable approximation, the dynamic generators of the static correlations between age and either component of party identification can be readily understood in such terms. Let me say for the last time that demonstrations of such compatibility fall well short of hypothesis confirmation as the latter is commonly construed; and my own scenario has little more than plausibility to recommend it, although I think it has at least that in some depth. But the important point is that most cohort analysts of party identification have approached these data with little more than competing simple-effect models in mind, and have still come to contradictory conclusions. Therefore complexity and indeterminacy are at best very indirect sources of the difficulties.

Sweeping back over the variety of problems upon which we have elaborated in preceding chapters, it seems to me that a considerable number have rather little to do with the intricacies of cohort analysis per se, but instead are familiar woes of secondary analysis much more generally speaking. Perhaps difficulties in strict logic cannot be placed in such a bin, although they are scarcely peculiar to cohort analysis, either. But some problems arise because secondary analysts, usually with limited to nonexistent experience in the nitty-gritty of mounting large-scale national surveys, are far less sensitized to the known procedural frailties of this or that specific data collection than were the original investigators, or are more naive about sampling error. Other problems arise because analysts become enamoured of a variable in an archived series, but do their work upon it despite only sketchy familiarity with the literature reporting past work on the behavior of the variable, and hence fall into interpretations that are most questionable in terms of other things already known. None of these classes of problems is any monopoly of cohort inference, although they account for much of the babel of conflicting verdicts.

Let us set all of these problems aside, in order to focus on one or two that are indeed more or less peculiar to problems of cohort inference as such.

In a recent paper, Glenn (1975) organizes a contrast between two types of tactics for the conduct of cohort analyses. One involves sophisticated regression analyses of cohort tables, using the suggestions of Mason et al. (1973) concerning minor artifices which can be employed to outflank the identification problem and arrive at a reasonable isolation of life-cycle, cohort and period effects. Knoke and Hout have provided the chief published exemplars, including the party identification analysis (1974), although other manuscripts abound. The competing tactic involves more traditional data inspection through simpler methods, and covers much of the remaining cohort analysis literature. Glenn appreciates the power of the newer methods, but feels that they lend themselves to a variety of abuses. He cautions that simpler methods will often reveal properties of the data that go unnoticed or are assumed away in advance by more massive, "black-box" data reductions.

I am sympathetic to numerous of the Glenn critiques. Given the whole thrust of this book, my preference for a good deal of inspection of the gross contours of a body of cohort data before even beginning more formal quantitative analyses should be apparent (see Chapter 2). Similarly, I agree whole-heartedly that around attitudinal materials, interactions between age and period impacts are not only conceivable, but are actively to be expected (see Chapter 4). Thus more elegant models which are only constructed to examine additive effects may produce misleading results, although of course modifications of those models are within reach. On the other hand, more casual inspection has had its abuses as well. Given the ease with which life-cycle gains in party identification strength were located with simple methods on a very short time series twenty years ago, or the clarity with which they pop out of the more elegant Knoke and Hout data, the intervening failure of a great spate of literature to find them with "simpler methods" is no very impressive advertisement. Surely, a sequencing of procedures from simpler inspections of a reconnaissance sort to more incisive large-scale data reductions after appropriate and inappropriate assumptions have been sorted out, is in order.[1]

However, one problem which has created substantial mischief in past cohort analyses of party identification within both styles of attack, and which is somewhat specific to cohort inference as such, is a lack of sensitivity to the issue of periodization, in nearly a historiographic sense. To develop this subject even briefly must carry us back into the central issues of cohort analysis.

We have already noted that there are rather asymmetric conceptual relationships between the three elements of the classic triad of effects, generation, life-cycle and period. Thus, for example, from one point of view it is the life cycle which is odd man out in the triad. This is true, as we have emphasized before, because of the high likelihood (but not certainty) of numerous continuities between period impacts and generation effects. From another point of view, it is the period effect which is odd man out. Both generation and life-cycle effects by definition refer to constancies in patterning either by birth year or by stage in the life span. The essence of the period effect, however, is change.

Such change may be simple or complex. In the simplest case, a period effect is no more than the new addition of some constant to the otherwise-constant generational and life-cycle patterns. In the most complex case, the erstwhile constant patterns of main effects and interaction terms between generation and life-cycle effects are changed as part of the "period" intrusion.

If the world were such that no constancies whatever marked either generation or life-cycle effects or their mutual interactions—that all of these terms were a new throw of the dice at each observation point—cohort inference would be impossible but it would not matter much since in such a world the subject would have no intellectual interest to begin with. In other words, not only the potential tractability of cohort analysis, but also its value as an intellectual exercise, rests on the presence of some constancy, over some observable term, in its underlying "process parameters." All cohort analysis mechanisms implicitly or explicitly assume that at least some such minimal constancies exist.

There is, however, an enormous gulf between a hypothetical world in which no relevant constancies exist, and one in which all relevant terms are eternally constant. Presumably the real world lies somewhere between these extremes.

While no cohort analysts of party identification would make the eternal constancy assumption, virtually all proceed in a fashion which assumes that at least for the period which available data cover, the critical process parameters are constant. Yet if an historian were to regard graphs such as Figure 1 and Figure 10, his first reflex would undoubtedly be to "periodize" them. Thus he would divide the span covered in Figure 1 (the direction component) into two subperiods, pre- and post-1965. And he would likely partition Figure 10 into three subperiods: a Depression-related transition, with a "before" period and an "after" period. We need not imagine that he would perform such a partitioning to facilitate cohort analysis. But in our immediate vocabulary, it would seem plausible to imagine that such an act of periodization would have the effect of maximizing the likelihood of within-period constancy of underlying process parameters, or, to put the matter another way, of minimizing the intrusion of the nastier (more complex) forms of period changes.

The likely benefits of such an act for meaningful cohort inferences should be obvious. Yet out of a total of nearly a score of published and unpublished cohort analyses of party identification that I have reviewed in the past fifteen years, only one (Glenn, 1972) has exercised such a partition to clarify an analysis.[2]

This is not to say that omnibus cohort analyses calculated across obviously heterogeneous subperiods necessarily generate pure nonsense. In fortunate cases, there is no reason why they might not be an excellent estimate of the configuration of "averaged" effects over the changing scene involved.

Indeed, this is much the way in which I view the Knoke and Hout (1974) estimates of the three-ply effects for both the strength and direction component of party identification. The estimates are surely in perfect congruence with everything I have learned from my own cohort data file, unlike some other conclusions arrived at by looser methods. However, they are best understood as a function of the particular mix of periods which happen to have entered into the calculations; and one can say with considerable confidence that had the mix of periods happened on been otherwise, the configuration of estimates would change very considerably. Unfortunately, the investigators do not make this time-specificity of their conclusions entirely clear.

In working from six presidential election studies between 1952 and 1972, the Knoke and Hout (1974: 707) estimates for the strength component of party identification places life cycle at the top (.0061 of variance explained, net of all other sociostructural and demographic factors); birth cohort second (.0055); and period third (.0029). Let us imagine instead that the investigators had conducted the same analysis on data from the six presidential elections from 1944 to 1964, thereby excluding the variance which is rapidly building up in the cohort and period columns in the post-1965 period, while gaining no compensating new variance from the elderly part of the spectrum. Then quite predictably the cohort and period values would wither notably while the life-cycle contribution would if anything increase slightly (because the shrinkage in total variance should proportionally outrun the shrinkage in the variance "explained" by life cycle). This would rearrange the values considerably, and match them quite nicely with our own estimates from the pure "steady-state" period.

Or alternatively, instead of imagining that the investigators had happened on a body of data collected eight years earlier, we can imagine they had access to data collected eight years later, or the six presidential elections between 1960 and 1980. Barring the very unforeseen in 1976 or 1980, they should now find period and especially cohort values dramatically increased, with the latter probably outrunning life-cycle effects.

A comparable thought experiment can be conducted with their estimates of relative contributions to variance in the direction component. Exactly what would happen to the large period contribution is not entirely clear without foreknowledge of the incidence of landslide elections, but this contribution is not of much interest in any event (see Chapter 5). Again barring the unforeseen emergence of a new realignment between now and 1980, the birth cohort contribution could be expected to decline slightly by 1952-1972 relative to a 1944-1964 data, and more sharply again for a 1960-1980 data base.

It may seem distressing that even estimates of relative cohort contributions as well-honed as those provided by Knoke and Hout also turn out to be so narrowly period-bound. It would be pleasing if one could make more timeless statements about a relative hierarchy of contributions to each of the components of the party identification variable. However, the time stream of reality definitely appears to be "lumpy" in these regards, and our assessments may as well reflect this lumpiness. Indeed, the whole concept of period impacts implies such a lumpiness across time. It may well be that the life-cycle contribution to the strength component is the only reasonably continuous input to the situation, although even this possibility deserves more careful reassessment after the current anti-party tides have quieted down.

The most important point of all this for the tactics of cohort analysis is simply that if distinctive periods are obvious in a cohort record, they might as well be recognized explicitly in the conduct of final data reductions. Partitioning into the obvious subperiods cannot guarantee that within subperiod, underlying process parameters are constant, or that there is a simplication of likely effects. One can surely build underlying models whereby key process parameters change, even disjunctively, without leaving so much as a distinctive ripple in more manifest indicators like the time path of marginal distributions. However, the fact that such confections are possible is a poor excuse for not attending scrupulously to such subperiods when in fact they *are* obvious in the record. If we are destined to deal at best in likelihoods and plausibilities where cohort inference is concerned, then this is a simple way to play the odds intelligently.

Such advice may not be of very general utility, since cohort analysts may well encounter many interesting series that fail to display period intrusions that are as oppressively obvious as they are in the case of both party identification components. If in closing I were to be forced on to the most general level, I would merely stress the crucial importance of the richest possible accumulation of side information in the formative stages of any cohort analysis.

Such an exhortation does not differ in any noteworthy way from what Glenn (1975) has in mind in calling for cohort analyses conducted with greater "insight." Nor does it differ notably from the Mason et al. (1973) dictum that "strong theory" should inform the selection of more specific analytic models for cohort investigation. If I prefer the term "side information," it is because it seems more capacious, certainly including both insight and strong theory, but including a great deal more as well. The fact that no large data-collection machines achieve very proper samples of the population cohort aged twenty-one through twenty-four scarcely rates as a creative insight, and to call it a piece of "strong theory" would be unimaginable. Yet it is just another piece of highly relevant information which can make a signal contribution to a more robust set of cohort inferences.

If I have tried to say anything at all unusual about the role of side information in the illumination of cohort inference, it is that some of the most pregnant "side information" need not lie very far "outside" the cohort table itself. The manifest evidence for subperiods is perhaps a central exhibit for this contention, but other examples have been strewn through these pages as well. It is my conviction, furthermore, that the sheer lengthening of available cohort series will in itself produce a constantly enriching lode of critical side information of this internal sort, since what is established as plausible within one subperiod can yield indispensable side information for the cohort analyses of other periods. However, all side information is welcome, and may often become unexpectedly pivotal.

To speak in praise of more information rather than less in the development of cohort inquiries runs very close to inveighing against sin. All inquiries profit from greater information. But it is the special lurking indeterminacy of the cohort inference problem that serves to raise the premium on such information to uncommon heights, and makes the message less trivial.

NOTES

1. This is, of course, no different from the cautious and well-informed applications advocated by Mason et al.

2. Almost none of these accounts even mentions the problem. Abramson (1976) does express concern about the diversity of periods involved, but this concern does not arrive at any noteworthy fruition in either his operations or his main conclusions.

Appendix A

PROPERTIES AND PECULIARITIES OF
THE COHORT DATA BASE

As reported in the text, the file of cohort data on which this essay is based was drawn progressively from twenty-nine national samples of the adult American population conducted by the Survey Research Center between 1952 and 1975, and contains over 40,000 individual-level observations. The file has some peculiarities and some marginal impurities. While to the best of my knowledge none of these features has significant bearing on any of our substantive conclusions, it is good form to make them clear.

(1) While all of the studies employed are strict probability samples, there is occasional variation as to the universe of American adults sampled. The vast majority of the studies are standard cross-sectional samples of the electorate. The chief variant involves a handful of early studies drawn from the Economic Behavior Program, in which the universe was limited to heads of

households. We have been unable to find significant differences
in the cohort behavior of party identification along these lines,
however. Naturally, the proportion male is much higher in these
samples than in the standard sample, which invariably under-
estimates that proportion by one degree or another. On the
other hand, we know of many examinations of party identification that attempt to compare males and females, with none
yielding noteworthy differences.

(2) The file contains a small admixture of cases (1958, 1960 and
1974) which were parts of panel studies, and hence do not rank
from one point of view as independent observations, although of
course the relevant measurements were taken at well-spaced
points in time. Since these reinterviewed people were only a
subset of their respective cross-section studies to begin with,
they make up less than 7 percent of the total bulk of the file,
and again there is no obvious reason to imagine that their
longitudinal observations are inappropriate additions.

(3) Although all election studies in the file, as well as a majority of
nonelection studies, provide age codes by year, some few of the
earlier studies used collapsed age codes. These studies were
added to the file by the expedient of dividing case numbers
across the single years according to a "normal" distribution for
that cohort, and assuming that the party identification distribution for the total wide cohort (usually, five years "wide")
applies to each artificial single year within it. This loses a bit of
temporal resolution in the early part of the file, but the problem
is not major.

(4) The most charming peculiarity of the file is that it is not
computer-borne or manipulable. The first third or more of it
was organized when programs were written in machine language
and their social science use was rare. It is far less cumbersome a
file to manipulate than might appear, since the basic unit is the
age cohort, with aggregate distributions across each party
identification category registered by annual cohorts in a
double-entry system organized alternatively by (a) birth year;
and (b) chronological age. It takes only an hour or so to log in
the results from any new study, and certain running totals are
kept which make monitoring what is going on quite simple.

The drawbacks to such a file are obvious. Being hand-manipulated, it is subject to a higher level of error than one would expect of a computer. I have always used an ornate system of double-checks to keep errors at a minimum, and I do not think the error rate is dangerously high, but it would be ridiculous to pretend there is no increment at all.

The most serious drawback is the inability to disaggregate the file in any other terms—by region, race, political involvement, or any other variables of interest. Whenever I have questions of this sort, I naturally turn to cohort data from the ICPSR archive, giving up the weight of the extra studies in my file.

Naturally, there is no reason why this file could not be put on tape, and I would be glad to do so for anyone who would pay cost. However, the transfer to tape would not in itself solve the problem of the inflexibility of the file for other disaggregations, since as noted, the organizing unit is the annual cohort, rather than the individual observation.

EXPLANATORY NOTES FOR FIGURE 1: "AGGREGATE LEVELS OF PARTY IDENTIFICATION STRENGTH"

A large number of editorial decisions was necessary for the construction of Figure 1. While we cannot review each of these in detail, we can summarize the general "policies" which produce the figure.

Treatment of SRC-CPS Data. Although twenty-nine discrete samples underlie this trend, some collapsing of adjacent time points has been carried out, so that only nineteen observations are charted. The collapsing was done quite deliberately to remove stray sampling bounces associated with some of the smaller single samples, and thereby to achieve a smoother curve. Such a tactic was avoided, of course, within extended intervals of real time populated by only a single study, even if it were small (cf. 1966). In one instance (1953-1954), two studies executed as much as twelve months apart were combined, chiefly because one of the two studies had less than 1,000 effective cases (cases of some substantive party identification report). Otherwise, all combined studies lie within an eight-month span, and most spread over six months or less.

The studies are located along the abscissa according to their relatively exact location in real time. That is, if the field work for a study in the summer of 1962 had a median interview data of July 15, then the observation is placed just past the midpoint of the year. While median dates of interview were not available for all studies, the dating can nowhere be in error by more than two months, and the majority are quite exact. When adjacent studies were combined, the location chosen was the N-weighted mean of their respective medians.

Values plotted on the ordinate follow from our customary method of summarizing distributions of identification strengths. The entry is a simple mean based on a scoring of "3" for strong identifiers; "2" for "weak" identifiers; "1" for nonidentifiers who nonetheless confess some "leaning;" and "0" for both staunch independents and those few "apoliticals" who profess a total lack of relationship to the political system or its parties. While such an averaging of clearly ordinal data has its known drawbacks, it is far preferable to the information loss entailed by imposing dichotomies arbitrarily at any of the three possible cutpoints; and virtually all of the work reported here could be carried out with comparable results, although only very awkwardly, with the scale treated ordinally.

Treatment of Gallup Data. We have made no extensive effort to accumulate Gallup data. The trend shown is based on accessible published tables, and is known to be quite incomplete. Points plotted up to 1964 are based on published summaries by Glenn (1972), and have undergone some adjustment for sampling inadequacies. For more recent points, where greater time precision seemed important, we have depended on distributions published in the *Gallup Opinion Index* or the *New York Times.*

It is to be stressed that the Gallup values plotted are entirely synthetic ones, adapted from published percentage distributions to fit the requirements of Figure 1. That is, the Gallup political affiliation item does not attempt to differentiate strength of party identification (see discussion in text). It produces instead a dichotomy: those who do and do not choose a party. The values calculated for Figure 1 assume that this dichotomy at least resembles the relevant dichotomy in the SRC-CPS measurement, among those who do and do not choose a party in response to the initial (somewhat different) probe, before the details of strength are measured. These two dichotomies are equated, and then the two Gallup categories are further artificially subdivided according to parameters suggested by the subsequent SRC subdivisions, in order to produce a four-category response which is then scored as for the SRC data.

This imposed subdivision is straightforward up through 1964, a period in which the proportion "strong" among the party choosers, and the proportion "leaning" among the nonchoosers, appears to have been temporally constant, to within a reasonable approximation. After that point, for reasons made evident in Figure 1, these two parameters become time-dependent. As the center of gravity of the strength distribution shifts toward the independent status, the proportion "strong" among choosers also secularly declines. In the early period after 1964, the proportion "leaning" among all nonchoosers actually increases to a maximum about 1969, and then also recedes. There is nothing peculiar about the initial increase. It conforms with what happens when water is sloshed through an ice cube tray. Since the vast majority of respondents (about 80 percent) were choosers before 1965, as strength dwindled overall the relative size of the "stronger" of the two nonchoosing categories was first inflated, before the flow continued on to the weaker (pure independent) category. For the post-1964 period, estimates of this time-dependence were produced, and applied appropriately to the gross Gallup dichotomies. One corollary of this whole procedure, of course, is that whereas two Gallup proportions published for 1967 and 1971 may be identical (in stray cases), the later value plotted in our figure would be somewhat weaker nonetheless.

It is worth noting that no further adjustments were levied in the plotted Gallup values. They are exactly as they emerged from this blind, mechanical rescoring process. Although they do more often than not show slightly higher values than the corresponding SRC-CPS observations (and the two curves could be fitted more closely if this "methods" discrepancy were adjusted away), the similarity in values remains impressive.

Treatment of the NORC Observation. In addition to item calibration problems, handled along the same lines as for the Gallup data, the 1944 NORC election study must be further adjusted to take account of the fact that it only referred to a white male universe. The value plotted in Figure 1 depends on the assumption that since white males in 1944 responded tolerably like white males in the later 1952-1964 period, the remainder of the electorate in that year could have been expected to respond to a party affiliation question as these other segments were in fact responding as of 1952, some eight years later.

BIBLIOGRAPHY

Abramson (1976)
Paul R. Abramson, "Generational Change and the Decline of Party Identification in America: 1952-1974," *American Political Science Review*, 70 (June, 1976), pp. 469-478.

Baltes (1968)
P. B. Baltes, "Longitudinal and Cross-Sectional Sequences in the Study of Age and Generation Effects," *Human Development*, 11 (1968), pp. 145-171.

Burnham (1965)
Walter Dean Burnham, "The Changing Shape of the American Political Universe," *American Political Science Review*, 59 (March, 1970), pp. 7-28.

Burnham (1969)
Walter Dean Burnham, "The End of American Party Politics," *Transaction*, 7 (1969), pp. 12-22.

Campbell et al. (1960)
Angus Campbell, Philip E. Converse, Warren E. Miller and Donald Stokes, *The American Voter*, New York: Wiley, 1960.

Carlsson and Karlsson (1970)
Gosta Carlsson and Katarina Karlsson, "Age, Cohorts and the Generation of Generations," *American Sociological Review*, 35 (August, 1970), pp. 710-718.

Cohn (1972)
Richard Cohn, "On Interpretation of Cohort and Period Analysis: A Mathematical Note," in Riley et al. (1972), pp. 85-88.

Converse (1969)
Philip E. Converse, "Of Time and Partisan Stability," *Comparative Political Studies*, 2 (July, 1969), pp. 139-171.

Crittenden (1962)
John Crittenden, "Aging and Party Affiliation," *Public Opinion Quarterly*, 26 (1962), pp. 648-657.

Crittenden (1970)
John Crittenden, "Reply to Cutler," *Public Opinion Quarterly*, 33 (Winter, 1970), pp. 589-591.

Cutler (1970)
Neal E. Cutler, "Generation, Maturation, and Party Affiliation: A Cohort Analysis," *Public Opinion Quarterly*, 33 (Winter, 1970), pp. 583-588.

Glenn (1972)
Norval D. Glenn, "Sources of the Shift to Political Independence: Some Evidence from a Cohort Analysis," *Social Science Quarterly* (December, 1972), pp. 494-519.

Glenn (1975)
Norval D. Glenn, "Some Cautions Concerning Statistical Attempts to Separate Age, Period and Cohort Effects," paper presented at American Political Science Association meetings, San Francisco, September, 1974.

Glenn and Hefner (1972)
Norval D. Glenn and Ted Hefner, "Further Evidence on Aging and Party Identification," *Public Opinion Quarterly*, 36 (Spring, 1972), pp. 31-47.

Gregg and Simon (1967)
L. Gregg and H. Simon, "Process Models and Stochastic Theories of Simple Concept Formation," *Journal of Mathematical Psychology* (June, 1967), pp. 246-276.

Jensen (1968)
Richard Jensen, "American Election Campaigns: A Theoretical and Historical Typology," paper read at the Midwest Political Science Association meetings, 1968.

Kish (1965)
Leslie Kish, *Survey Sampling*. New York: Wiley, 1965.

Klecka (1971)
William R. Klecka, "Applying Political Generations to the Study of Political Behavior," *Public Opinion Quarterly* 35 (Fall, 1971), pp. 358-373.

Knoke and Hout (1974)
David Knoke and Michael Hout, "Social and Demographic Factors in American Political Party Affiliations, 1952-1972," *American Sociological Review*, 39 (October, 1974), pp. 700-713.

Mason et al. (1973)
K. O. Mason, W. M. Mason, H. H. Winsborough and W. K. Poole, "Some Methodological Issues in Cohort Analysis of Archival Data," *American Sociological Review*, 38 (April, 1973), pp. 242-258.

Mannheim (1952)
Karl Mannheim, "The Problem of Generations," in *Essays on the Sociology of Knowledge*, Paul Kecskemeti (Ed.), London: Routledge and Kegan Paul (1952), pp. 276-322.

Mueller (1970)
John E. Mueller, "Presidential Popularity from Truman to Johnson," *American Political Science Review*, 64, No. 1 (March 1970), pp. 18-34.

Mueller (1971)
John E. Mueller, "Trends in Popular Support for the Wars in Korea and Vietnam," *American Political Science Review*, 65 No. 2 (June, 1971), pp. 358-375.

Nie, Verba and Petrocik (1976)
Norman H. Nie, Sidney Verba and John R. Petrocik *The Changing American Voter*, Cambridge, Mass.: Harvard University Press, 1976.

Riley (1973)
Matilda White Riley, "Aging and Cohort Succession: Interpretations and Misinterpretations," *Public Opinion Quarterly*, 37 (Spring, 1973), pp. 35-49.

Riley et al. (1972)
Matilda White Riley, Marilyn Johnson and Anne Foner, *Aging and Society*, Vol. 3: *A Sociology of Age Stratification*. New York: Russell Sage Foundation, 1972. (Especially Chapter 2 and Appendix for cohort analysis materials.)

Ryder (1965)
Norman B. Ryder, "The Cohort as a Concept in the Study of Social Change," *American Sociological Review*, 30 (December, 1965), pp. 843-861.

Schaie (1965)
K. Warner Schaie, "A General Model for the Study of Developmental Problems," *Psychological Bulletin*, 64 (1965).

INDEX

ABOUT THE AUTHOR

PHILIP E. CONVERSE received his M.A. in sociology in 1956 and his Ph.D. in social psychology in 1958, both from the University of Michigan, where he is presently Robert C. Angell Professor of Political Science and Sociology. He has been the recipient of several honors and awards, among these memberships in The American Academy of Arts and Sciences (1968) and The National Academy of Sciences (1973). Dr. Converse has served in executive and advisory capacities in several research associations. Among the most recent are The National Science Foundation and The Social Science Research Council. He has authored many articles for scholarly journals, primarily on such topics as the formation of public opinion, electoral behavior, and partisan attitudes. His books include: *The American Voter* (John Wiley, 1960; with Angus Campbell, Warren E. Miller, and Donald E. Stokes); *Social Psychology: The Study of Human Interaction* (Holt, Rinehart & Winston, 1965; with Theodore Newcomb and Ralph Turner); *Elections and the Political Order* (John Wiley, 1966; with Angus Campbell, Warren E. Miller, and Donald E. Stokes); *The Human Meaning of Social Change* (Russell Sage Foundation, 1972; ed. with Angus Campbell); and *The Quality of American Life* (Russell Sage Foundation, 1976; with Angus Campbell and W. Rodgers).